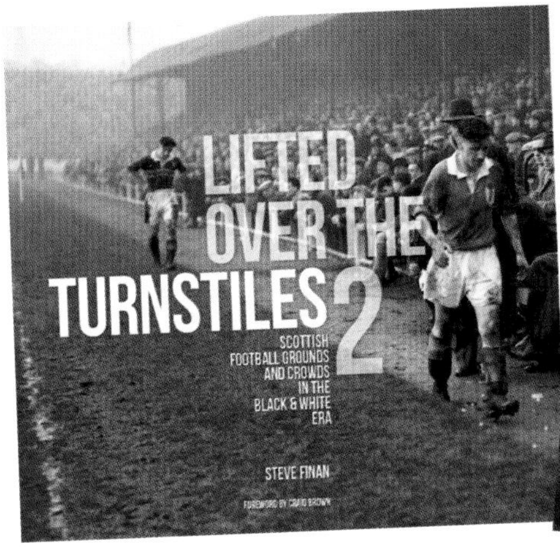

BY STEVE FINAN

There are two linked volumes of these latest Lifted Over The Turnstiles books, with Scotland's teams spread equally over them. To purchase the other volume go to: www.dcthomsonshop.co.uk

Volume 3: ISBN 978-1-84535-890-7

First published in Great Britain in 2021 by DC Thomson & Co., Ltd., Meadowside, Dundee, DD1 9QJ.

Compiling these books has been the most enjoyable and rewarding task of my working life. I am immensely proud of them. I therefore dedicate both books to the most important people in my life, my wife, daughter and son – Carole, Rebecca and Lewis Finan.

COVER/BACK COVER DESIGN | LEON STRACHAN

Typeset, internal design and composition by Steve Finan (proudly a hot metal compositor 1979-83).
This book is set in Times New Roman regular/bold/italic 13 point on 15.6 point leading.

HAMPDEN PARK

Introduction

OVER the course of working on these two books, a roughly four-year process, I found myself being re-taught how to look at a photograph.

It was an odd experience, because I thought I already knew how to look at a photo – I reckoned it was a simple matter of opening your eyes!

But it isn't. Or at least that's not all that happens. That's not quite how people look at photos of places where they used to go with their family and friends to watch their team play football.

They see different things. They see their lives.

There is a huge measure of pride mixed up in it. To criticise an old football ground in front of a supporter of that club, is every bit as bad as saying "What an ugly bairn" about their offspring.

So I had "tests" done on all the individual club chapters. I consulted the experts – those who went to those grounds week after week all those years ago.

I usually had the luxury of several options on which photos to use, so asked my test readers whether this or that photo was better? Whether a pic of the stand, the terrace, or the outside of the ground should be shown?

I was taught to appreciate that every step of terracing, every perimeter fence, every crush barrier is important to someone. It is the barrier they stood in front of when their grandfather leaned on it from the other side. Or the track-side wall they were barely tall enough to peek over when first taken to the fitba with their big brother.

People notice the tiniest of details – like the shape of the girders holding up a roof, the thickness of a barrier that might be (or might not be) easy to sit on. Or the way a stand seat quickly tipped up and might trap a juvenile finger.

There is real emotional investment in these photos. They are parts of family history.

They notice these things because they lived them. The details became part of "that" game, when their cousin (hilariously) got his finger nipped, or when their dad shouted a few choice (and funny) words while leaning on "that" barrier.

I grew to love personal stories like that. I came to greatly enjoy hearing about the history attached to these photos – not just information about the games that are shown being played, goals scored, or the players on view, but the stories of the people who went to the games and stood on the terraces.

There are thousands of football books that talk about the game. There are far too few that properly examine the experiences of the supporters.

My foreword writers also deserve mention.

Craig Brown knows as much as any man alive about Scottish football stadiums. He has played at them all, managed at them all, and been a spectator (when he was the Scotland boss assessing candidates for the national team) at them all. He knows what he's talking about and generously shared his experiences in Volume 2.

For a foreword for this, Volume 3, I struck out in another direction. Where Craig is the voice of experience, Leanne Crichton is the voice of youth. But not just any voice. She is deeply involved in Scottish football on multiple levels, as a player, a coach and a journalist. She knows the game and she is a thinker.

She gave this book exactly what it needed – an opinion on Scottish football grounds from another angle. In her foreword she talks about the glimpses of history that can be seen at Scottish grounds, though old terraces might have long gone.

This is where I hope some real value can be found in these books for younger readers.

The record of a team's victories, trophies and players is one thing, the roots of the club, the places where the supporters stood, the old ground, the old glories, is quite another.

Most Scottish clubs are more than a century old. A lot of their character, their spirit, can be found in the history of their support and that is tightly tied to the history of their ground.

Lastly, as with Volume 2, I feel compelled to point out some of my favourite photos in this volume.

When you find a box of negatives that hasn't been opened for five or six decades, there is a feeling like you used to get when given a mystery Christmas present as a child. "Ooh, what is in this box?"

And often, there was something of real beauty.

I was greatly amused, and puzzled, by the Firhill vegetable patch on page 15.

All the photos of Real Madrid v Eintracht Frankfurt were amazing to find, but the training shot in an empty Hampden, on page 68, especially took my eye. Puskas looks every inch like he is where he was born to be – about to play one of the greatest matches of football history in the biggest stadium in the world.

Freddie Glidden at a packed Tynecastle on page 160 is a superb photograph, as is (in a different way) the bone-chilling cold apparent in Stenhousemuir v Cowdenbeath on page 294.

I have a fascination with floodlights and found the first Ibrox lights a compelling photo on page 110.

My favourite floodlights story, however, concerns St Johnstone striving to not upset the local gentry on page 138.

I have to admit being (in my quiet way) very proud of these books. I greatly enjoyed putting them together. I hope you can share my enjoyment and enthusiasm for old fitba photos. Thank you.

Steve Finan, 2021.

Foreword, by Leanne Crichton

MY job with the BBC and my football career has meant that I visit and have played at a lot of Scottish football grounds. Often, I am struck by the history you can see.

It might be an entire stand that has stood for a hundred years, or just a few old concrete steps. It is fascinating to catch glimpses of how grounds used to be, even if it is just something that is behind or at the sides of the newer bits.

There is the old terracing still visible at the far corner of Tannadice, the 100-year-old stand at Cappielow and the grand main entrance to Ibrox.

The stands at Somerset Park, Firhill and East End Park have had some alterations but they also still have that look of "history" about them. You get a sense of it as you walk through them.

I've also been to Cathkin Park, what's left of it. And though Third Lanark were gone long before my time, you can still hear the echoes of what was once a proud football club. It is quite an emotional place to visit.

I wish I'd seen these places in their glory days.

And I wish I'd had the chance to commentate on the great games of history and interview the giants of the game. I wish I had played at these grounds in front of big crowds.

Most of all, I wish I'd experienced Hampden with a crowd of 130,000 or more inside it, voicing the Hampden Roar. I have spent ages looking at the Hampden photos.

It must have been a tremendous boost to the players to play with backing like that.

The crowds at Hampden is something I speak to my Nana about. She's 89 and widowed 34 years but she recalls my Papa going to those games – some a little more scary than enjoyable, but fascinating all the same. It would have been remarkable to play in front of, for sure

As time goes on, the old parts of the grounds are covered up, or ripped out, or clubs move away. It is progress, it has to happen.

But each new stand, each new ground, each, old bit covered over is a step away from what football used to be.

That's why I like this book.

The photos give a sense of the long history of football in Scotland.

When I look at the photos of Ibrox or Celtic Park,

places that have changed so much, I imagine those huge places as they once were.

I work out where the fearsome Jungle was in relation to the giant new stands, or how different Ibrox must have felt when the towering bowl-shaped ends curved away from each side of the main stand.

I think my favourite photos, though, are the ones with football action on the pitch in front of the crowds, with everyone standing and packed in together so tight. Incredible.

One of my favourite modern grounds is Tynecastle and it is fascinating to think of how it must have been with the old terraces and that L-shaped cover on the Wheatfield side.

Then, of course, there are the grounds that have entirely disappeared.

Some I recall a little, but I have spent ages looking at the photos of Brockville, Muirton, Broomfield and Boghead in this book and I think of all the highs and lows, great goals and great players, and the deep emotions these places must have seen.

You can't understand Scottish football, and what it means to people, without understanding what grounds mean to supporters.

They regard these places as their own home, not just their club's home.

I have to concentrate on the current game, that's my job as a player, coach and commentator. But anyone who has worked in football or watches football has to be aware of the history of the clubs and what that history means to the supporters.

So this book has an importance beyond a nostalgic look back.

It shows Scottish football and football clubs in their right and proper setting. They can be seen here with their history alive around them.

You get a sense of the long past that has led to now, the decades-long journey that supporters take with their club. The supporters deserve a lot of respect for the way they stick with their clubs through thick and thin. I think people inside the game sometimes forget things like that.

I learned a lot from this book and, importantly, I greatly enjoyed it.

Leanne Crichton, 2021.

CONTENTS

The grounds aren't in alphabetical order. This is designed as a dip-in-dip-out book with gems scattered throughout the chapters.

Things you don’t see any more

FOOTBALL has changed, I’m sure we’ve all noticed that. Going to a match 50 or 60 years ago was a very different experience to what it is today.

The lack of standing areas is the most obvious thing, of course. We all stood at games, and you had to be careful to position yourself with your tribe.

Sometimes you’d stand with the lads from your district, as you knew where they’d congregate.

Sometimes it became a choice of standing with the chanting hard core, or with the older blokes away from the melee, or (in your youth) among the kids learning to be fans who lined the track-side wall in front of the noisy section.

This last group spent as much time watching their hero supporters as they did watching their on-field heroes, and ambitiously added their high-pitched voices to songs that promised: “You’re gonny get your fucking head kicked in”.

Many of the old sights have died away. Things like blue invalid cars parked on the track.

Then there was the half-time scoreboard, filled in by gnomes from under the stand, who only ever came out to fulfil this purpose then scurried back to hide until the next home game (or so it seemed!)

You had to buy a programme to learn that a 0-1 alongside the letter K meant Cowdenbeath were winning at Stranraer.

Toilet rolls are no longer launched on to the pitch.

There was quite a technique to throwing them. You had to keep a hold of one end so it unrolled as it flew (this was in the days of tough, shiny, piles-irritating toilet roll, not the velvety chunky stuff you get today).

The toilet roll was supposed to mirror New York-style streamer-tape parades – though Scottish versions rarely reached such levels.

At Junior matches hordes of youngsters used to invade the pitch at half time and kick balls about in the dusty goalmouth. They savoured the sensation of shooting into an actual net as very few schools or Boys’ Brigade games were played with real nets.

And football smelled different. There was a beer, tobacco, urine, Bovril, pie grease, sweaty aroma that might be mixed with the stoor kicked up under covered terraces when a goal was scored. The Mount Florida end of Hampden was particularly dusty – your snotters were black for days afterwards.

The only types of food available were a pie, or almost completely flavourless chipsticks of highly questionable sell-by-date.

And where did all those stray dogs come from?

■ **Right: Shawfield, November 24th, 1973. Clyde 0, Rangers 2, Dogs 1. Keeper Phil Cairney has a hold of it, Clyde trainer John Watson is about to grab it, defender Jim Burns is offering advice to both of them.**

■ Dogs on the pitch used to be fairly common. The days when turnstiles were pieces of metal at roughly waist-height didn't only allow youngsters to be lifted over, they allowed passing dogs – attracted by the smell of pies and the chance to make thousands of new friends – to run underneath. The canine criminal on the left was nicked at Rangers v Hibs, September 5th, 1981. The cute pup (above, right) was apprehended by subby Harry Hood during a Celtic v Rangers League Cup tie on August 25th, 1973.

Left: Celtic v Dundee United, December 16th, 1978. Hamish McAlpine uses his big goalie hands to good effect.

Above: Of course, they always had to be a bit different at Shawfield. Clyde v Hearts, April 16th, 1966. The swan had probably flown in from the nearby Richmond Park pond.

■ Some dogs were at games legitimately. Rangers' Derek Parlane is entangled in the net during a 5-0 win at Motherwell on November 16th, 1974, attracting the attention of a police dog. These dogs used to patrol pitch-side tracks. The idea was that anyone attempting an invasion would have canine teeth sunk into their soft tissue areas. If this happened nowadays there would be a public outcry over the cruelty – some would defend the human rights of the invaders, others would wring their hands over the effect on the traumatised doggies.

■ **There appears to be a vegetable patch in this photo of Partick Thistle's Firhill, which is quite a rare sight at Scottish football grounds these days. The match is Cambuslang Rangers v Greenock Juniors in the Central League Championship Decider on June 4th, 1966. Greenock won 3-2. No potatoes were harmed during the playing of this game.**

The pale blue, single-seat, three-wheeler vehicles that used to line cinder tracks were called Invacars.

They had fibreglass bodies and were developed by engineer Bert Greeves, working with his paralysed cousin. The duo saw a business opportunity in the number of disabled former servicemen after the war.

Tens of thousands of Invacars were produced between 1948 and 1977. Later models had a 600cc engine, capable of 82 mph, though there were always stability issues. Many tipped over on a tight corner. Most were recalled in 2003 due to safety concerns.

This is the 1966 Scottish Cup Semi-Final between Celtic and Dunfermline, at Ibrox. Celtic, in their all-green strip, won 2-0 in front of a 53,900 crowd.

■ **Left: The half-time scoreboard being filled in at the rear of Pittodrie's south terracing in 1967.**

■ **Right: March 12th, 1977. Young Dundee fans stage a mini pitch invasion (complete with thrown toilet roll) after Eric Sinclair scored late in a Scottish Cup Quarter-Final v Arbroath.**

Gayfield hosted a crowd of 9,558 that day, but Dundee won 3-1.

Arbroath's Gordon Marshall (the former Hearts, Hibs and Newcastle keeper) doesn't have a number on his shirt – though that was common for goalkeepers at the time.

But with modern squad numbers it is something else you rarely see these days.

■ Gaun yersel, wee man! Celtic v Airdrie, October 15th, 1966 – a young pitch invader takes to the field, pursued by a member of Glasgow's finest.

■ Soon he is apprehended and brought back to dad. Charmingly, throughout all of this the game carried on regardless.

■ You don't see paddling pools sunk into the Ibrox pitch to amuse Bobby Shearer and Johnny Hubbard any more. This was the steeplechase water-jump still in place after the Ibrox Sports of 1958.

They called the brown leather ball, with a lace where the inner bladder was inserted, a “tub”.

This one is pursued by 23-year-old Pars striker Alex Ferguson in the Third Lanark v Dunfermline game of April 10th, 1965.

Balls were stipulated to have a circumference of 27 to 28 inches, and weigh (when dry) 16 to 18 ounces. These regulations were made in 1872, and are still in place.

Top-quality tubs were made of leather from the rump of a cow, cheaper ones were made with harder leather from the shoulder. First Division games were supposed to be played with the softer balls, but this didn’t always happen.

Sometimes, managers left the ball soaking in a bath overnight if they thought their team were better suited to a heavy ball.

Gradual improvements, including water-resistant coatings, began to be introduced in the 1950s, but the first fully waterproof balls made of synthetic material weren’t seen until the 1960s and took a long time to become universally used.

■ **Thirds at Cathkin Park again. This is earlier the same season, September 5th, 1964, a 2-1 loss to Morton in driving rain (with a white ball). In those pre-segregation days, spectators moved around grounds and would, if needs be, seek shelter from the elements by all crowding under the one terrace with a cover. Crowds aren't allowed to move at most stadiums nowadays. This is the biggest single difference to the experience of being a spectator then and being one now. You used to be free to choose how you watched the game.**

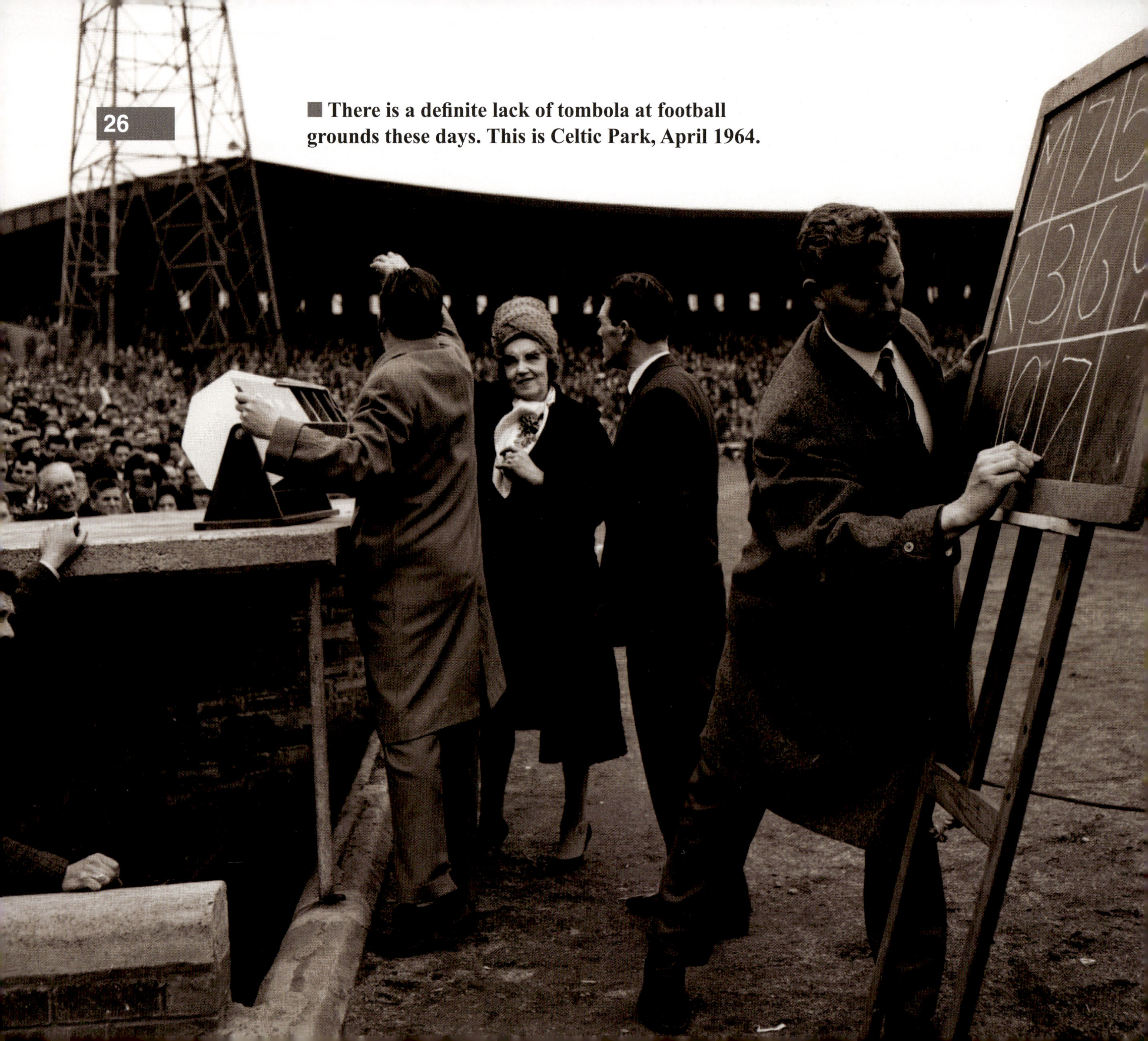

■ **There is a definite lack of tombola at football grounds these days. This is Celtic Park, April 1964.**

■ Honest-to-goodness, ankle-deep glaur! Dundee keeper Ally Donaldson caked head-to-toe in mud during the Clyde v Dundee match of January 18th, 1969. It was a 0-0 draw, but a cracking match full of incident and quite a few last-ditch sliding tackles. Pitches never seem to be in this state nowadays. In this photo the goal-line and six-yard-box line are barely visible in places.

■ **You no longer see injured players carried off on a stretcher that wouldn't be out of place at The Battle of the Somme, surrounded by a platoon of officious First Aid men who knew (and would tell you!) what an important job they were doing.**

The casualty was Hearts midfielder Jim Townsend, in a Scottish Cup tie at Celtic Park on March 18th, 1972. It was a 1-1 draw.

■ Ref A. F. McDonald delivering a ticking-off for snowball-throwing, while the crowd collectively puts on its best "wisnae me mister – a big boy did it and ran away" face. This was Morton v Rangers on November 20th, 1971, a 2-1 away win. Perhaps it is a measure of the respect given to referees of the time – the snowball barrage actually did stop! Weatherwise it wasn't a very nice day, even by Greenock standards.

You no longer see substantial square goalposts and crossbar, with iron stanchions to hold up a deep net – which was also kept in place by bits of string tied round the posts.

The net was pegged in to the grass, whereas nowadays it is attached to a weighted pole – which in turn is firmly fastened at ground level to prevent any chance of a ball squirming through.

Nets were made of the most durable twine that could be found, often (when it became available after the war) tough nylon that would last for years.

These nets made a satisfying whirring/ripping sound when a pile-driver shot hit at a certain angle. Nets today are softer, the same noise doesn't occur.

Nets started out as white, but as the seasons passed would become a chewing gum-grey.

Coloured, striped, or chequered nets in the home club's colours are a quite recent frippery.

The fashion nowadays is for aluminium posts, often ellipitical in shape. They make a clanging noise when goalkeepers kick them to clear turf from their boot soles. But to this day there is nothing in the laws of the game that prevents square goalposts – though they must be no more than five inches thick.

Corner flags used to be collected by ball boys, who raced to perform this task as soon as the final whistle sounded. The flags on these corner posts were patterned or coloured, or had words or letters emblazoned on them in a manner commensurate with the club's groundskeeping budget, or the skill of the manager's wife with a sewing machine.

Square goalposts were more prevalent in Scotland than in any other European footballing nation. Hampden, Ibrox and Muirton (to name but a few) had muscular goalposts/bar arrangements that could probably have doubled as anti-tank obstacles.

The Scottish penchant for these hefty-looking posts was, largely, because square-cut timber is cheaper to buy and easier to bolt together than circular or oval-cut timber.

Indeed, Scottish clubs often used to have their groundsmen make the posts themselves, with a saw, drill and coach bolts. Sometimes players would find this was one of the odd-jobs they were expected to do during the close season.

St Johnstone, towards the end of their time at Muirton, installed posts taken from the salvaged roof beams of Crieff Bus Station, where GS Brown (the construction firm owned by Saints supremo Geoff Brown) had been building houses.

They took these goals with them to McDiarmid Park. But this coincided with the SFA insisting on the removal of old fashioned full-length iron stanchions holding up the net, following the incident in February 1993 at the Partick Thistle v Dundee United game. Referee Les Mottram disallowed a Paddy Connolly "goal" that had hit the iron stanchion and come back on to the pitch.

Saints' general manager at the time, John Litster, resisted the SFA directive to get rid of the old stanchions on heritage grounds!

■ **Right: The square-cut goals at Ibrox, pictured in 1966.**

32

Scottish football grounds were situated in residential areas in the heart of our towns and cities.

Left is Raith Rovers' Stark's Park in 1957, half-back Jackie Williamson going through his paces with the houses on Kirkcaldy's Pratt Street close behind.

Nowadays, many grounds' surrounding houses have been demolished. But for a century or more there was almost always people living close to grounds. Often in the most common Scottish city dwelling, the tenement.

This helped nurture a phenomenon seen regularly among football fans that was given a name by Professor Yi-Fu Tuan (the leading light in the high-fallutin'-sounding discipline of "humanistic geography"). He called it topophilia – a love of place.

Topophilia is an attempt to explain and measure the affection human beings feel for buildings, streets, areas and, of course, stadiums.

Fans hold traditions dear, and love their old ground. That is why you are reading this book. It doesn't matter if the ground is scruffy or decrepit. Loyalty for "home" leads supporters to vigorously, sometimes irrationally, defend it as "the best" in arguments.

Fans regard players, managers and owners as transient, while the stadium is the constant. It is difficult to separate whether they love club or stadium more.

Placement is, clearly, crucial to this.

In Scotland it is rare for a club to move, rarer than in any other major European footballing nation. St Mirren are the biggest club to have done so recently. But if it is to be done, "to where" is the paramount question.

We haven't embraced Continental and American ideas of mixed-use stadia suburbs with fan plazas, shopping malls and hotels surrounding the "ballpark".

The majority of big English clubs who have built new stadiums moved less than a mile and to a city site. Arsenal's hop from Highbury to The Emirates was very short and widely accepted. Leicester City's move from Filbert Street to King Power Stadium was 200 yards.

However, West Ham United's four-mile shift to the London Stadium was a matter of some angst.

In Scotland, St Mirren moved in 2009, but just along the road. Falkirk's 2004 flit from Brockville to the Falkirk Stadium wasn't a long way, neither was Broomfield to Excelsior for Airdrie. Hamilton Accies' old and new Douglas Parks are a goal-kick apart.

The exceptions are Clyde, who were homeless after leaving Shawfield, moving 15 miles to Cumbernauld. And Livingston who travelled even further, from Meadowbank to West Lothian – but as part of a transition of identity rather than a simple relocation.

It isn't always possible to find a nearby inside-the-city site so some new-build stadiums in the UK have been in parkland areas or industrial estates.

These settings give a very different feel. Where once the surrounds were tenements, pubs and shops there are factory units or even countryside.

Invariably, "soul-less" will be shouted by fans which is unfair as, going back 140 years, most stadiums were built on city outskirts but the city grew to envelop them.

But still, sometimes, a move could be the better option and many big Scottish clubs have contemplated a flit, though few have actually gone through with it.

Some – Aberdeen and Dundee among them – are to move soon. Down south, Everton have firm plans.

No club can do it without serious consideration and strenuous efforts to win the approval of their fans.

We no longer experience the sight and sound of massed pipes and drums marching up and down the Hampden pitch before Scotland games.

This was a World Cup Qualifier against Sweden, on September 9th, 1981. Scotland won 2-0.

Pipe bands stirred the heart. They were intrinsically Scottish.

It was a much better idea than American rock music played over the PA system so loud you can't hear what the person next to you is saying.

If I could change one thing about the experience of being a spectator at a modern football game, it would be to ban the aural assaults delivered by some (but not all) clubs' PA systems.

Bring back the pipe bands, or let the crowd build the atmosphere itself. The way it used to be.

Please.

Celtic

THE main stand at Celtic Park was opened on August 10th, 1929, with a 2-1 win over Hearts.

Built by Glasgow company Duncan & Kerr. it isn't an Archibald Leitch stand though the designer, David Mills Duncan, was Leitch's chief draughtsman before setting up his own company.

It became the main stand after what was known

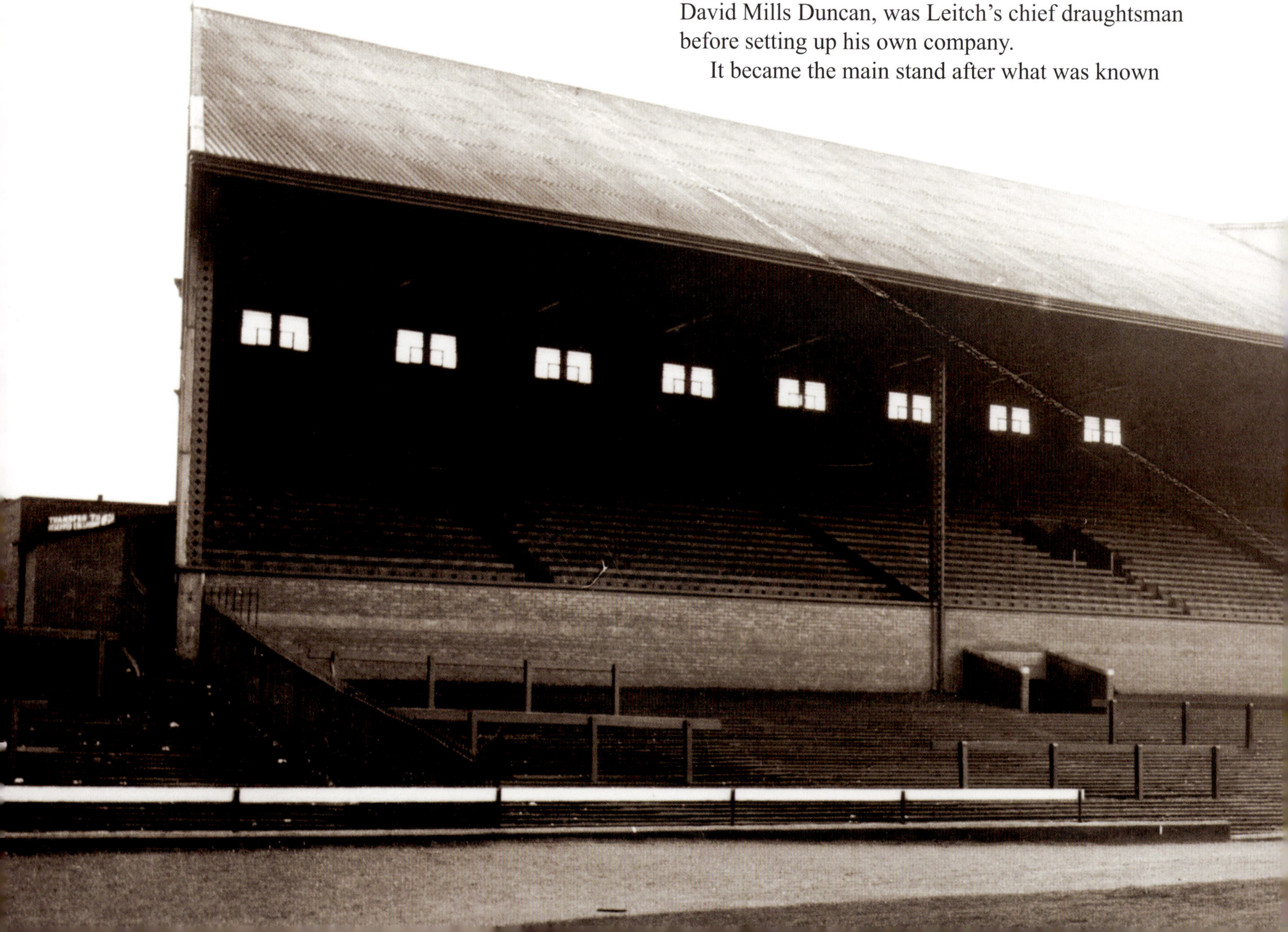

as the Grant Stand, built in 1899, which had been a revolutionary building, was demolished. It seated 2,000 and had a fully glassed front – though the windows were prone to misting-up.

When the replacement stand was being built, Celtic had to play a few games at Shawfield. This wasn't because of the work, it was because the pitch was trodden down and had debris strewn across it after a fire in the old pavilion (on the north side, where The Jungle would be) where players had changed and the admin offices were.

The £35,000 1929 stand was, by the standards of the time, a luxurious place to watch football and the subject of a great deal of praise.

On the day it opened, Celtic manager Willie Maley personally came out to organise a photo of the Hearts and Celtic players together in front of it, while a band played Auld Lang Syne.

The 5,000-seat 1929 stand remained until the re-build of 1971. At that point the roof was replaced and the main seating deck was extended at both ends and down over what had been the enclosure.

38

Celtic Park's record crowd is sometimes quoted as 92,000 for a Rangers game on January 1, 1938. This probably isn't accurate. It was more likely closer to 83,500 (another of the figures mentioned at the time). But almost 100,000 had turned up for that game.

More than 10,000 were locked out, with police horses used to control the queues at the turnstiles. Kick-off was six minutes late, giving police time to "settle" the crowd.

There were 50 people injured due to crushing.

At least one barrier collapsed and crowds spilled on to the track at several places. Willie Maley came out to appeal to people to stay clear of the pitch.

There was such an exuberant pitch invasion at the end that Celtic's Callum McDonald ("Malky" who went on to manage Killie and, briefly, Scotland) had to be rescued from the crowd around him by police and appeared "dazed by the thumping" from all the pats on the back and head after the home side's great performance in a 3-0 win.

The Sunday Post of the time claimed: "There was a larger proportion of women than usual at the game, and many of these fainted and had to be attended by St Andrew's Ambulance men."

It also listed the men who were taken to hospital, along with some details of their injuries:

Robert Lawson, 1920 London Road, Glasgow (severe abdominal and chest injuries). William Gallacher, 28 Robinson Avenue, Greenock (suffered from crushing). John McCann, 174 Mathieson Street, Glasgow (injury to ankle). Thomas Roe, Doncaster Street, Glasgow (injury to ankle). Five other men injured are Henry Irvine, John Hunter, Thomas Whiteside, John McMonagle, and James Ramsey, all of Glasgow.

The Jungle was probably the most famous, or infamous depending on how you looked at it, "shed" in Scottish football. Its influence is still felt today.

It is pictured on this page prior to its 1966 re-build, and on the next page on the first day it welcomed fans to stand on the newly concreted terraces under the new roof for a friendly against Manchester United.

The old roof had been in place, with little change, since 1907 and was long past needing attention.

The old place was dirty and smelly and the barrel roof leaked badly. But it held a special place in the hearts of supporters, and legends of it are still told.

As a structure, it certainly wasn't perfect. The terracing was wood-edged compacted ash and earth, and weeds grew during the summer. When Celtic scored, the dust storms were choking.

The roof supports meant supporters had to carefully choose their place to have a clear view of both goals.

The roof didn't quite cover all of the terracing, there were about six steps at the front that were open to the elements.

But then, no one expected it to be perfect. Going to stand in The Jungle wasn't about comfort.

It wasn't a fathers-and-bairns type of place either. It was very crowded for big games, with a lot of violent movement depending upon the ebb and flow of the game and atrocious – or hard but fair – tackles (depending on who was getting in about who) on the pitch.

The toilets were, to put it mildly, primitive. It was

well known that you stayed clear of the yellow rivers. Some say they recall seeing ladies' toilets in the 1950s, though others swear there never were such things.

Jock Stein was said to often be frustrated with The Jungle, due to its inhabitants' tendencies to be quick to criticise players.

Jock also reckoned the state of it was a symbol of the clubs' neglect of itself in the 1950s and early 1960s and pushed chairman Bob Kelly hard to spend money on the 1966 upgrade.

It was finally demolished in the great rebuild of Celtic Park in 1994. Progress had to come, of course.

However, the tradition of The Jungle is still apparent. The raucous atmosphere that was generated has been retained. There is an expectation of noisiness of the fans going to Celtic Park. Their fathers and grandfathers were loud in The Jungle, the current fans carry on in the same fashion.

This makes for an atmosphere famous throughout Europe. It is an asset to Celtic and can be traced directly back to the days under that old leaky roof.

The Jungle spirit lives on.

■ Celtic Park held 60,000 for the visit of Manchester United in August 1966. The Jungle's TV gantry wasn't added until later.

The 1952 New Year Old Firm match at Celtic Park was a violent day. Bottles were thrown, fights broke out, the pitch was invaded, and after a slew of arrests two men were sent to jail for their actions.

Glasgow magistrates called a meeting and made several "recommendations", one of which was that "any flag or emblem which had no association with football or Scotland" should not be displayed.

It blew up into quite a confrontation.

Celtic, with backing from Rangers it must be added, refused to take their tricolour down, saying it was part of the club's heritage and had been a gift from Ireland's Taoiseach Eamon de Valera.

Celtic chairman Bob Kelly insisted there was nothing in the long-established SFA rules that mentioned flags and his club, which had flown the tricolour for more than 30 years, therefore had a watertight legal case.

Yet spectator bans, a hefty fine, even expulsion from the league were threatened as punishment.

The matter became a power struggle, with the SFA even suggesting Celtic should agree to take down the flag in recognition of the SFA's authority, but not actually take it down. The SFA would then review their original decision and rescind it.

Unsurprisingly, Celtic didn't agree to this.

The flag remained in place and the arguments petered out.

■ Happy days at Celtic Park.

September 4th, 1971, club president Bob Kelly's wife gets a kiss from Jock Stein before raising the 1970-71 Championship flag from the alleyway that ran up the side of The Jungle.

Sir Robert would die less than three weeks later, the end of an era for the club.

Incoming Celtic chairman Desmond White, a former Queen's Park goalkeeper, looks on.

Celtic were about to play Clyde, and would win 9-1 with a first League goal for a young man named Kenneth Mathieson Dalglish.

■ **Celtic Park 1966. In an era of more common-sense policing (before stewards) lassies sitting on the perimeter wall with their feet on the track wasn't seen as a major public order incident.**

However, a phalanx of policemen can be seen further back in the crowd – probably making an arrest.

■ October 30th, 1965. Ball boys parade the League Cup around Celtic Park at half-time of a 6-1 League defeat of Stirling Albion. Celtic had beaten Rangers 2-1 at Hampden the previous week.

■ **John Hughes and Bobby Murdoch carry John Divers, with the much-complained-about holes in the old Jungle clearly visible.**

■ Left: May 15th, 1982. Celtic had just beaten St Mirren 3-0 to confirm the 1981-82 Championship. The Celtic Park main stand makes an impressive backdrop to Danny McGrain hoisting the trophy, with a young David Moyes in the No.12 shorts. Visible on the main girder of the stand is one of the retractable supports (there is an identical one on the other side) which swings down and is bolted in to place to bring extra stability to the roof.

■ Above: November 6th, 1971. The stand roof had only been in place for a couple of months by this point and, as can be seen, there are no swing-down supports. This was a matter which resulted in legal action. The stanchions have only been used during a handful of games (they interfere with the view) when extreme snow, rain or high winds are expected. Though they are often deployed when games aren't being played.

■ **Neil Mochan leads his Celtic team-mates down the battered-looking terrace steps at Celtic Park in a 1950s training exercise.**

In 1967 Celtic displayed the trophies the club had won so far that season (this was before Lisbon).

They are, from top, the Glasgow Cup, League Cup and Scottish Cup.

In those days the League Championship trophy was awarded to the winning club's representative at the League AGM.

Green-and-white towels on the littered terrace of the old main stand enclosure is an unusual setting for showing off honours, but provides us with a close look at the old-fashioned concreted steps.

There aren't many examples left of such terraces.

The dotted indentations were made with a spiked roller on wet concrete and were intended to make the steps less slippy on a rainy or frosty day.

■ Celtic v Clyde, May 1, 1971. The last time the 11 Lisbon Lions ever took to the field in a competitive game. It coincided with a big day in the history of the Celtic Park stand, which was being demolished. The normal tunnel was out of use, so the teams emerged from where the spectators' entrance to the enclosure had been.

Goalkeeper Ronnie Simpson came out and warmed up with the Lions on what was an emotional day, but had a shoulder injury and didn't actually play in the game. Evan Williams took over in goal. "Faither" is shown making his way back up the enclosure steps just as the game kicks off. Celtic won 6-1.

Celtic v Penarol, August 2nd, 1973 – the Uruguayans, champions of South America, played to a 35,000 crowd as part of an 11-game European tour.

Two of the famous "Three Kings" (Matt Busby, Bill Shankly and Jock Stein) in the same place at the same time.

Jock had invited his friend to Celtic Park for the glamour friendly and the club made a presentation to mark Shanks' 15 years as manager of Liverpool.

Not a man who suffered shyness, Shankly saluted the cheers of the crowd in his native land, with The Jungle chanting his name. Jock had to gently persuade him off the pitch to allow the game to start.

Celtic Park, that Thursday evening, played host to one of the greatest gatherings of managers ever seen in Scotland.

Also present were Tommy Docherty (Manchester United), Don Revie (Leeds United), Bob Stokoe (Sunderland), Joe Mercer (Coventry City) and Jack Charlton (Middlesbrough).

GRATI

■ This is Celtic Park on September 1st, 1954. A league game against Dundee. Jock Stein shepherds the ball back to his keeper, with Dundee's Albert Henderson trying to get a look-in.

It is many years since Jock died, and even longer since he pulled on a jersey and took to the field at Celtic Park.

Few alive today can remember when he played.

But his presence, his legacy, still defines the club, the style of play shown by the team on the pitch, and the standards of behaviour in and around Celtic Park.

A potent argument on any Celtic matter would still be: "Jock wouldn't have stood for that."

Three legends of the Scottish game: *Scotsport* commentator Arthur Montford, Celtic's Danny McGrain, and The Jungle, with its distinctive long, unbroken lines of crush barriers.

This was March 25th, 1978, Jock Stein's last Old Firm game as Celtic manager.

Arthur had been doing commentary on the match (a 2-0 Celtic win) that had just finished.

An announcement was about to confirm that Danny's ankle injury, sustained in a game against Hibs the previous October, was likely to keep him out of the Scotland squad for the forthcoming World Cup in Argentina. A sad loss to the nation.

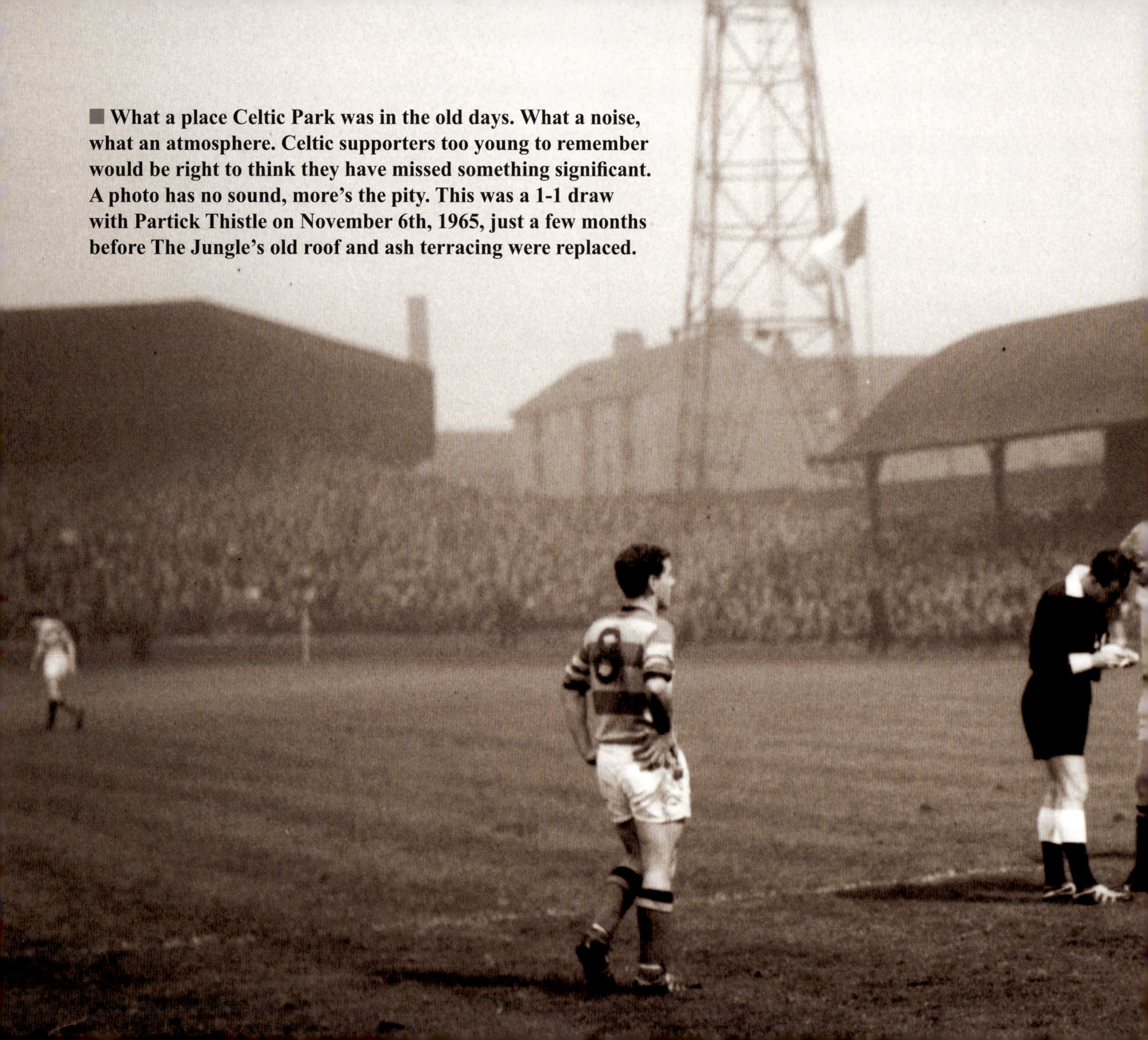

■ What a place Celtic Park was in the old days. What a noise, what an atmosphere. Celtic supporters too young to remember would be right to think they have missed something significant. A photo has no sound, more's the pity. This was a 1-1 draw with Partick Thistle on November 6th, 1965, just a few months before The Jungle's old roof and ash terracing were replaced.

One of the great things about football stadiums, and one of the reasons they have such a hold over our affections, is that they were where we saw our heroes.

The fans got to know their personalities, their strengths and weaknesses.

Celtic Park has seen more than its fair share of characters.

Charlie Tully (right, cracking a joke at training) would be up there with the best of them. Jimmy Johnston (left, in a game against Hibs on December 11th, 1965) would be high on the list too.

These men gave their hearts to Celtic Park. The thousands who watched them gave their hearts right back.

However, the old Celtic Park was about more than football (although good football was always important). Going there had an extra dimension. It was a social thing. It was an expression of a culture.

And the men who became real heroes, the real Celtic men, had a spark, a twinkle in their eye, a wee bit devilment, an inbuilt desire to entertain.

The old Celtic Park was sometimes a little bit ragged around the edges. But it had its own personality. It had a soul.

Perhaps you had to experience it to fully understand it.

Hampden's greatest ever game

ON May 18th, 1960, the fifth European Cup Final, was contested at Hampden between Spain's Real Madrid and West Germany's Eintracht Frankfurt.

A crowd of 127,621 (still a record for a European Cup Final) saw a quite incredible game.

Real won 7-3 with a display of attacking football that enthralled the crowd and the 70 million watching on television around the world.

Most of these photos have lain unseen over the six decades since then.

■ **Ferenc Puskas scores Real Madrid's third.**

Madrid, led by Puskas, train at Hampden. The scene was set. The two best teams in Europe, in the greatest stadium in the Northern Hemisphere, about to play one of the most celebrated games in world football history.

This was the first time a Northern European club had made it to the final. The Germans were Oberliga Sud (Southern League) champions as these were the days before the nationwide Bundesliga was formed. Play-offs between the five West German regional champions decided who represented the country in Europe.

A handful of German and Spanish supporters followed their teams to Glasgow but the majority of the crowd were Scots – and a lot of them thought the Frankfurt side would win.

Eintracht had thrashed Rangers in the semis by an aggregate of 12-4. It was 6-1 in the Waldstadion, then 6-3 at Ibrox. Though Real were the bookies' favourites, many across Scotland reckoned any team that could score a dozen against Rangers must be in with a shout.

With the Scottish view on football, we reckoned that an impressive gathering of German manhood would out-muscle, out-run, and just swat aside the fancy-dan Latins despite all their flicks and tricks. Erwin Stein, the Eintracht centre-forward, was a formidable athlete.

But it didn't work out that way.

Among the crowd were an 18-year-old Alex Ferguson, and the then Dunfermline manager Jock Stein. The game had a lasting effect upon both those men.

So what did they see?

The football was highly innovative, though to a modern eye the defensive work (especially the marking) is loose, and the efforts by full-backs to prevent crosses coming in is unremarkable (to be kind).

Madrid showed a fluidity of movement that wasn't often attempted in those days of rigid formations. They lined up as (roughly) a 3-3-4 with Alfredo Di Stefano in the middle of the park. But he moved across the pitch to whichever side the ball was on, and rhythmically exchanged short passes with his full-backs or wingers.

Madrid didn't, as almost every British club at the time would do, fire long balls from the keeper up to a tall centre-forward. They built from the back, though the defenders quickly fed the ball through to the midfield to bypass the German forwards.

They did, however, launch lightning attacks from corners against them. Francisco Gento played no defensive role but positioned himself for a throw-out from keeper Dominguez, if and when he got the ball.

Their play in the last third was recognisably of its time as they exploited the searing pace of Gento, who would put conventional crosses into the box.

But at times Di Stefano would orchestrate a frontal advance to the edge of the box, exchanging short passes with Puskas and Luis del Sol.

It was a type of football half a century ahead of its time. A Pep Guardiola side playing in the style of that 1960 Madrid team wouldn't look out of place.

It was only possible because the players in the side were supremely comfortable on the ball.

What is often forgotten is that three Madrid players (Pachin, Gento and Di Stefano) were in the Spain side that beat England 3-0 more than 1,000 miles away in the Bernabeau just three days before this final.

The football they played at Hampden was the talk of Scotland. There were many calls for us to learn lessons.

■ **Right: The Germans played the same XI that had beaten Rangers at Ibrox.**

Renowned Scots ref Jack Mowat conducts the coin toss.

Di Stefano, aged 33 at this point, gets his own and his team's first goal.

■ Di Stefano gets Real Madrid's second goal.

■ **Puskas tucks home the fourth from the penalty spot, into the quaintly many-times-mended Hampden net.**

Puskas heads home the fifth from a Gento cross.

■ Then Puskas got the sixth.

And Di Stefano puts the seventh past the long-suffering Egon Loy.

■ It was the all-time highest-scoring European Final. A hat-trick for Di Stefano, four for Puskas. No player has scored four in a European Cup or Champions League Final since.

The score could have been a few more. Madrid hit the post, and had several other close things.

And that Los Meringues side wasn't just Puskas, Gento and Di Stefano – all 11 on the pitch were full internationals. Eight for Spain, one Argentinian, one Brazilian and one Hungarian.

The shot creeping narrowly past the post in this photo was from Brazil winger Canario.

The manager of Real Madrid is listed as Miguel Munoz. But much of the in-depth coaching was done by Emilio Ostreicher, the Hungarian "general manager".

He had been boss of Honved and a major figure behind the Magical Magyars' football of the early 50s. He was out of the country at the time of the 1956 Hungarian uprising and stayed away.

Ostreicher brought Ferenc Puskas to Spain and is sometimes said to be the real brains behind the run of five European Cups that Real Madrid won, 1956-60.

The Real Madrid players embarked upon a lap of honour, cheered to the high heavens by an appreciative Hampden crowd.

The leading Scottish football writer in 1960 was Jack Harkness, the Wembley Wizards goalie who played more than 300 games for Queen's Park and Hearts before a career in sports journalism.

The weekend after the final, in a *Sunday Post* article titled "Throw the rule book in the Clyde", he gave the Scottish football establishment both barrels:–

Today, the footballers of Real Madrid are back basking in the sunshine of Spain. With the cheers of Hampden's 127,000 still ringing in their ears. The players themselves were flabbergasted by the terrific reception they received at the end of Wednesday's European Cup final.

They told me their football had been appreciated all over the world, but no audience ever "let its hair down" like this Glasgow crowd on Wednesday night.

I hope, too, those cheers are still ringing in the ears of everyone connected in any way with Scottish football.

It was six years ago that I first discovered that outside these islands a new type of football was being played. Since then I've travelled the world sending home warning despatches about how our own game was being left behind.

The cheers of these 127.000 football-loving fans on Wednesday were surely a condemnation of the men who paid no heed.

Let's recap to the 1954 World Cup in Switzerland. My final report from Berne, following Scotland's 7-0 defeat by Uruguay, read: "An emergency meeting of the S.F.A. must be called immediately. The Hungarians, the Germans and the Latin Americans have so improved on our ideas of football that in a few years their game will be quite unrecognisable from ours."

No post-mortem was held. At the next S.F.A. meeting, an official announced that Scotland's venture in the World Cup had been a financial success. And we had learned a great deal.

Onwards now to the World Cup of 1958. Remember how, although some folk thought we were in an easy section, we didn't win a game in Sweden. Not one official member of the Scots party remained behind for the final stages, or to inquire why the game in other countries was going forward at the same rate as our own game was going back.

My final despatch from Stockholm was headed: "Too proud to take a tip." Again, I asked for an emergency meeting of the S.F.A. Again, it was in vain. Again, nothing was done.

Today things are different. The football fans of Glasgow have demonstrated that this "new" football is what they want.

So the honest truth is that Hampden Park on Wednesday night actually left Scottish football with a crisis on its hands. A crisis that affects legislators, club officials, players, and the spectators themselves.

1. The Legislators. We must have smaller leagues without shutting down any of our smaller clubs. No one wants to kill off the Stranraers, the Brechins, the East Stirlings. But they should be allowed to find their own level, leaving the big outfits to set their own houses in order.

More important still, we must sweep away all the outmoded rules that stand in the way of progress.

Why bring Puskas or Di Stefano over to teach our schoolboys (as has been suggested) if our clubs can't take these same schoolboys under their wing? Every first-class club in Europe or Latin America has countless boys in its membership. They just laugh at our system.

The S.F.A. should throw the rule book into the Clyde and leave the clubs to get on with their own jobs.

2. Club officials. For a spell they should stop demanding results at any price. They should not hesitate to go to the Continent for top-line coaches. Turn your backs, gentlemen, on the tough-tackling "hero" and give preference to the ball-worker.

3. The players. There has been far too much hero-worship in this football oyster of ours. The adulation heaped upon what are really very ordinary players has some of them strutting around as if the clubs who pay them are actually lucky to have their services.

Recent results, I hope, will have brought them back to earth. The big frogs in the wee pool have surely discovered they are actually gey wee frogs in a big pool.

4. Spectators. On Wednesday night you cheered both teams. Come August you'll be shouting on your own team to "get stuck into them so-and-sos". That approach to the game must stop. The spectator has as vital a part to play as any.

Start the season with your minds still focused on what you saw last Wednesday. And give all your encouragement to the fellows who are really trying to emulate it. If you must get something off your chest, vent all your wrath on the fellow who's out to stop the ball-worker at any price.

Wednesday, May 18, was a historic night for Scottish football. Is it too much to hope, I wonder, that it could also be the date on which Scottish football pulled its head out the sand?

St Johnstone

MUIRTON PARK'S biggest ever crowd came when St Johnstone weren't in Scotland's top league. It was a 29,972 attendance for a Scottish Cup Second Round tie against Dundee on February 10th, 1951.

The Saintees might have been in the "B Division" (as it was called at the time) but were going well in fourth place, challenging for promotion.

There was a good travelling support from down the Tay but the game caught the imagination of the Fair City and most of the crowd were behind the home team.

Saints went ahead after only 90 seconds when Jackie Malloch stabbed home an Ian Brydon knock-down from a corner. Muirton went daft.

The final score was 3-1 to Dundee in what was a a close encounter throughout, that might have been closer still if Saints' outside-right Brydon hadn't been injured after 20 minutes and became little more than a limping passenger.

To be fair, Dundee's South African half-back Ken Ziesing also got an injury that left him an on-field spectator in the second half. It was a further 16 years before substitutions would be allowed.

■ The main stand was opened with the ground in 1924, with the ice rink overlooking the North End built in 1936. A roof was added to the East Terrace in the early 1960s, and floodlights were installed in 1964.

■ **January 2nd, 1971. Aberdeen's visit brings out very healthy 25,000 crowd but there was trouble in the ice rink end. Whether these are Aberdeen lads or members of the Perth Pack being lifted is open to speculation. The Dons won 1-0 on a frosty pitch.**

Lager SKOL Lager
BELLS SCOTCH WHISKY BELLS
BELL'S
SHAVERS
SKOL-Top o

It made financial sense to make the move to McDiarmid Park in 1989 and St Johnstone have reaped the benefits of a modern stadium. They are now established among the elite of the Scottish game.

But Muirton had character and when packed full it generated a wonderful atmosphere.

The high segregation fence under the East Terrace shed was paid for by Aberdeen in 1988. Muirton's capacity was restricted to 5,000 at the time, with only a waist-high fence separating fans. But when Saints drew The Dons in the Cup, the Pittodrie club paid for a new fence which satisfied crowd control requirements and the police agreed to raise the attendance to 10,000.

It instantly paid off, with thousands making the trip down the A90.

The canny Dons, taking half the gate receipts, benefited too – and won the game 1-0.

■ **Saints v Rangers on November 2nd, 1974. A bumper crowd watches Rangers fight back from 1-0 down at half-time to win 2-1. Muirton was a cauldron of noise that afternoon – the dust clouds under the shed roof were never so thick.**

■ **Muirton now lives only in old photos and the memories of supporters of a certain age. This photo was taken in 1983, just as Saints were about to win Division 1.**

Airdrieonians

BROOMFIELD is long gone. It was famous for its pavilion, built in 1907, which was the last of its kind in Scotland and survived until the ground itself closed in 1994. Broomfield, as everyone said, was too small, run-down, and not fit for modern-day football. But it is still sadly missed by older fans.

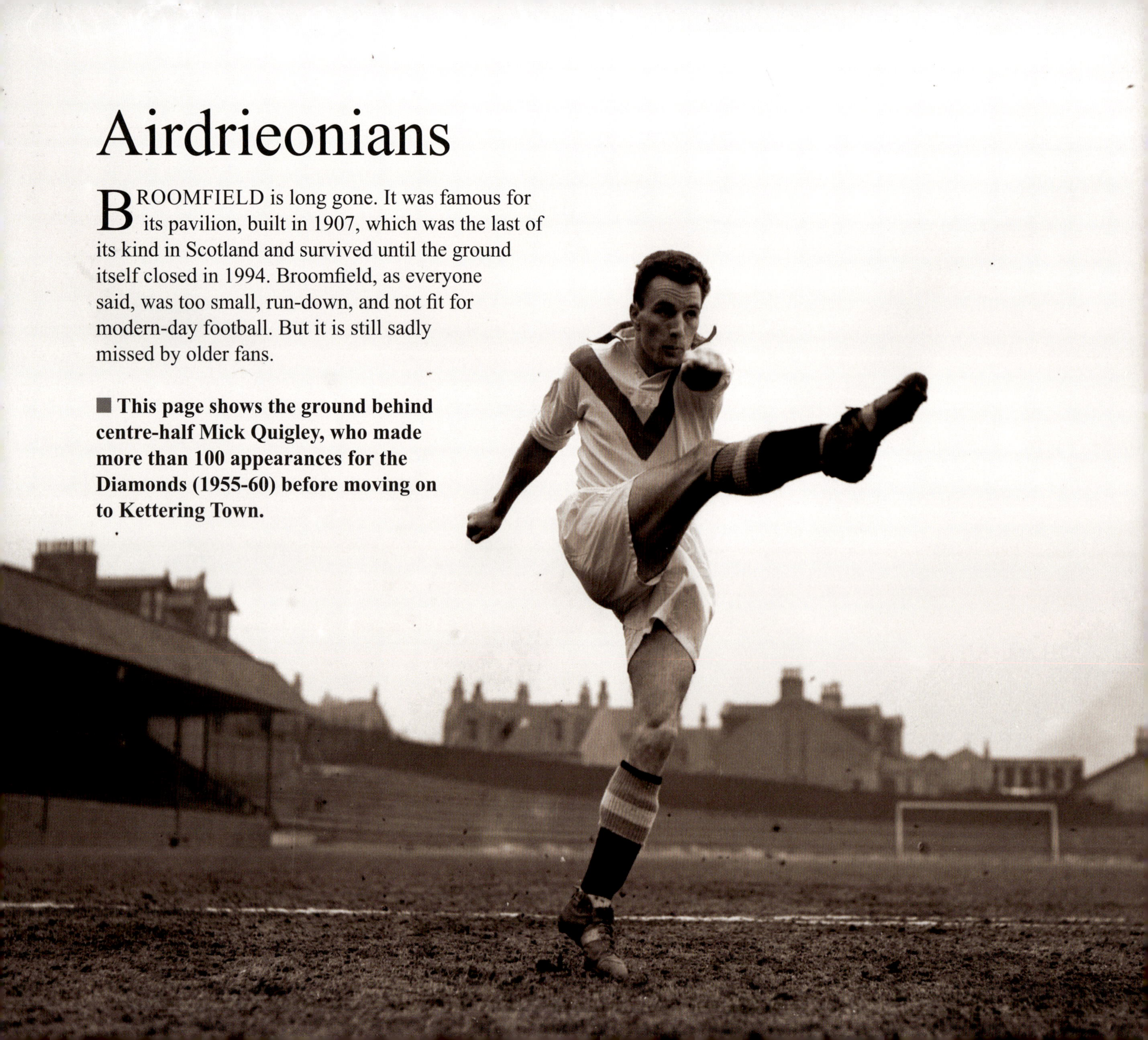

■ **This page shows the ground behind centre-half Mick Quigley, who made more than 100 appearances for the Diamonds (1955-60) before moving on to Kettering Town.**

■ **Tommy Duncan's handstand antics give a better view of the far end of Broomfield, with its unusually broad steps – almost sloped platforms as much as they were a traditional football terrace.**

Broomfield's biggest crowd is, frankly, a mystery. In an era of uncertain counting at turnstiles at almost all Scottish clubs, Airdrie were among the worst offenders. They rarely managed to give accurate crowd figures.

The game usually cited as Broomfield's best-attended is a Scottish Cup Quarter-Final against Hearts on March 8th, 1952. But the crowd figure is an estimate.

There was, indisputably, a lot of people in the ground that Saturday. Hearts brought a massive travelling support who saw a highly entertaining 2-2 draw.

Airdrie were two up at half time (David Shankland and Ian McMillan), but Hearts' Terrible Trio team (though inspired on this occasion by a driving performance from right-half Freddie Glidden) fought back with goals from Willie Bauld and Alfie Conn to take the tie to a replay.

Newspapers at the time were at first informed the crowd was 24,000, with gate receipts of £1,680. But the club later gave the attendance as 26,000. Neither of these very round figures will be entirely correct.

There may have been well over 26,000 at the game. There were several instances of incursions on to the pitch, and spectators were five-deep all round the track.

The replay the following Wednesday at Tynecastle attracted a quite remarkable 40,528 for a 3.30 pm midweek kick-off. Hearts won another cracking game 6-4.

■ **This photo shows yet another pulsating Scottish Cup tie. Airdrie's Jimmy Docherty gets between Morton's Gordon Thom and Jimmy Whyte to score the home side's first goal in a fightback to draw 3-3 (after being 3-0 down with 16 minutes left) on February 10th, 1951. To no one's surprise, the crowd for this game wasn't recorded.**

The layout under the stand at Broomfield was unique in Scottish football. There weren't dressing rooms or offices – these were in the pavilion.

The undercroft of the stand was a darker, quieter place. There were passageways to get to the seats and, in later years, a door out to the social club at the rear of the stand.

The low angled spaces under the seats were murky storage areas containing rollers, mowers and other groundskeeping equipment. There were sandbags for the odd occasion when the park was flooded, and frost covers for winter.

Legend has it that when the stand was demolished, in one of the gloomier corners an ancient trophy was found that no one could identify.

■ **Jimmy Welsh is beaten to the ball by Celtic keeper Dick Beattie on August 24th, 1957. This was a League Cup section game, which Celtic won 2-1 in front of what was said to be a 15,000 crowd.**

Another photo of Mick Quigley, this time playing against East Fife. Broomfield got a roof on the terrace opposite the main stand in 1959, which would become home to the notorious Section B.

TEXACO
TEXACO
TEXACO
TEXACO
TEXACO
THE CAPOCCI MAN
CREAM

The terrace roof, with its distinctive TV gantry. This is v Celtic, September 25th, 1971, the day Airdrie paid £16,000 to buy Tommy Walker from Arbroath, a record fee paid to a Scottish Division Two club at the time.

■ On this page, and opposite, the Broomfield stand can be seen, with its leaning floodlights and unusual (very small) under-the-stand dugouts. The photo above is v Rangers, August 9th, 1980, the first Saturday of the league season. We enjoy looking back at great games of the past but they weren't always great – this one was a stinker, a 1-1 draw that barely stirred the interest even of those who had paid to get in. But this photo of Willie Johnston and John Greig making their way along the track gives a flavour of Airdrie in the early 80s.

■ **August 16th, 1969. Airdrie 0, Rangers 3 – a more entertaining afternoon. It was a hard-fought League Cup tie that was subject to the occasional torrential shower. The Diamonds' celebrated goalkeeper, Northern Ireland international Roddy McKenzie, is given treatment. Note trainer Adam Good's boots with their much-worn-down moulded studs. Every laddie who grew up in 1960s Scotland owned a pair of fitba boots with soles like that! The crowd was given as precisely 16,000, another Broomfield round number.**

Floodlights

NOWADAYS, even public parks have floodlights of superb quality. It wasn't always so.

Floodlights, or drenchlights as they were called, were put up (by most clubs) in the 1950s and '60s. As with everything to do with Scottish football, the advent of lights comes with a few ifs, buts, and maybes.

Stenhousemuir played Hibs in a friendly in 1951, often cited as the first "modern" Scottish game under lights. Modern is given quotes because there were various attempts to play under arc lights as far back as the late 19th Century.

The lights for that 1951 match barely qualified as floodlights (see next page).

One of Arsenal's visits, on December 8th, 1953 inaugurated the Ibrox lights, although they were put up a year earlier.

The first sanctioned floodlit League game was Rangers v Queen of the South on March 7th, 1956. Rangers won 8-0 and the race was on to light up football.

■ The archetypal Scottish floodlight in all its glory. This is Pittodrie's south-west pylon, pictured in 1980, rising as if part of the gasometer structure that used to loom over the ground.

As the timetable on page 128 shows, most of the bigger clubs were quick to erect lights. They went on roofs, pylons, or pylons on roofs.

No two clubs did it the same, or financed it the same way. The result was, and still is, a mish-mash of styles and quality. But the lights and pylons (or roof mounts) became an important part of every ground's character.

The switch-on was always treated as an occasion. Many clubs played glamour friendlies and put out souvenir programmes.

Floodlights opened the door to midweek evening games, but more importantly also to proper Continental competition. Northern European clubs couldn't play midweek games in winter until lights were installed.

Prior to the 1960s, midweek internationals took place on Wednesday half-holiday afternoons. Evening games against touring sides had to be in early or late season.

Famous encounters, such as Real Madrid v Eintracht Frankfurt 1960 – the year before Hampden's majestic pylons were erected – were only possible if played in the long evenings of summer.

The Stark's Park lights.

There is an enduring myth that Jim Baxter's transfer to Rangers paid for Raith Rovers' floodlights but they were erected, bought and paid for before his transfer in June 1960.

The funding came from the supporters' club (who donated £1,000) and a development association set up specifically to fund the lights.

If any transfer helped it was talented winger Jimmy McEwan to Aston Villa a year earlier – hence the invitation to Villa to inaugurate the lights in September 1960.

To the left of the stand is a piece of Scottish history, the winding gear of Seafield Colliery, which employed 3,000 Fifers in its heyday.

It was said to have enough coal to stay in production for 150 years but closed in 1988 after 28 years as a working mine. The pit head towers were demolished the following year.

The early lights at Stenhousemuir weren't, to be truthful, the brightest. But Stenny's ambition shone through strongly and deserves full recognition.

The club's committee proved a valuable point – floodlit football in Scotland was viable, and fans wanted to see it.

The lights had been at Ochilview for a while and were used for training, but there isn't a record of an actual game previously played under them.

The details of their origin are lost in the murky gloom of history, but they, or a similar array, may have been in place since the war. Local butcher Tom Douglas was said to have donated money to the club for lights and a sound system and there are reports of 1,500 locals dancing under the lights to celebrate VE Day in 1945.

The SFA gave a go-ahead for that first floodlit friendly against Hibs to take place on November 7th, 1951. Four portable lights were brought in to augment the 14 already in place.

It was all-ticket with a 7pm kick-off, and went down very well. Hibs, with their Famous Five forward line, put on a footballing masterclass and won 5-3 in front of 4,500 crowd. More than 8,000 tickets had been sold, but the night was foggy, so many thought the game would be cancelled.

■ These photos show a Warriors v Kilmarnock B Division game at Ochilview on March 21st, 1953. Ochilview's floodlights can be seen on their poles. Kilmarnock's rising star at inside-right, Willie Harvey, is focused upon because there was transfer speculation surrounding him.

Rangers then took over the floodlights torch in Scotland.

The Light Blues had played Arsenal under Highbury's newly-installed lamps in October 1951. And the Ibrox board, led by Bill Struth at the time, saw the light.

The first Ibrox lamps were on temporary roof-mountings (scaffolds would be a more accurate description) alongside low pylons. They are pictured here in a game against Hearts. There were 23 lamps on each scaffold, some of 1,000 watts, some 1,500.

The system was modelled on the lights of Yankee Stadium, New York.

Fans were invited to a trial match on November 26th, 1952, to see them and were charged 6d each that was donated to charity.

Rangers played a series of matches under these lamps.

A more permanent set were installed in 1953, mounted on the roof of the stand and the shed opposite, with the stand-alone pylons sold to St Mirren.

Every club in Scotland was taking note of these experiments, with boardroom discussions on how to emulate this bright step.

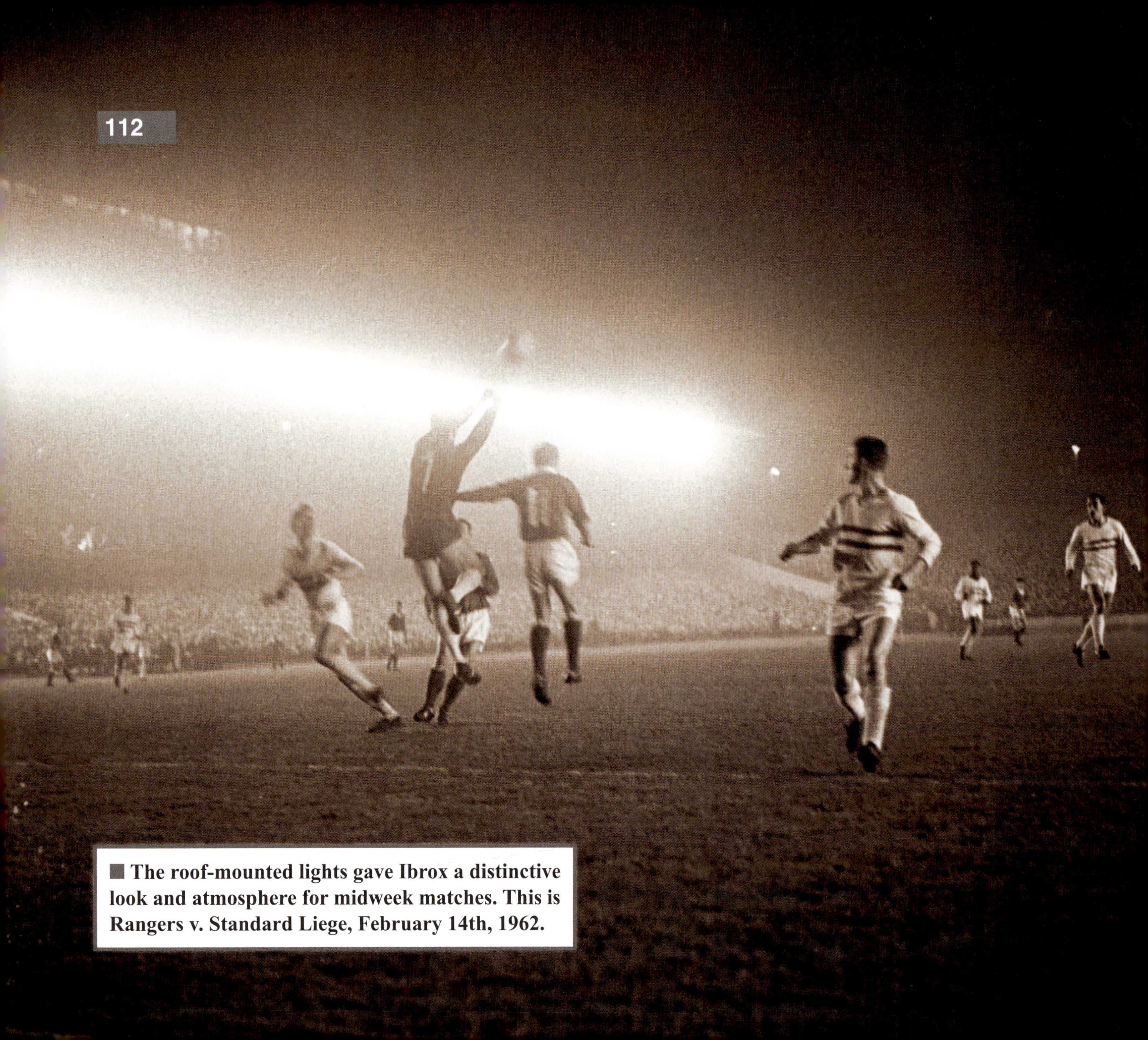

The roof-mounted lights gave Ibrox a distinctive look and atmosphere for midweek matches. This is Rangers v. Standard Liege, February 14th, 1962.

■ Ibrox got an expensive new set of lights in 1967, on roof-mounted pylons – making it the only ground in Scotland ready (in the words of newspapers at the time) for the “exciting arrival of colour television”.

■ **Fir Park's roof-mounted floodlights (left: behind Johnny Aitkenhead) were put up in 1956 and proved a great success, with Motherwell playing Leeds United in a series of floodlit friendlies. But the spindly fittings were damaged in a gale in January 1958 (as seen here, with 'Well's John "Chopper" McPhee trying to score against Partick Thistle). The club put up high pylons in 1960, with the old system sold to East Stirling for £500.**

116

Floodlights changed the game in Scotland and the look of our stadiums. They also changed the look of our cities.

Before multi-storey flats sprang up, floodlight pylons were among the highest structures in some towns, especially if situated away from the town centre.

Nowhere was this more obvious than in Dundee.

The pylon on the left belonged to Dundee United before being replaced with a shorter, cylindrical pole and roof-mounted lights in the 1990s. These lights were slightly higher (surely an attempt at one-upmanship) than those at Dens Park.

As is often commented upon, Dens and Tannadice are 100 yards apart on the same street. The fascination with this is regarded with some disdain in the city, where supporters have grown up with the grounds in their places for 110 years. The strangeness wore off a long time ago. But outsiders regard it as a novelty, and it does seem remarkable if you've never seen such a thing before.

Dundee is built on steep terrain, with its football grounds on the shoulder of the "Hulltoon" to the east of The Law that dominates the city skyline (again, only outsiders call it the "Law Hill").

So the lights of both grounds can be seen from miles out to the east and south-east, in the Angus and Fife countryside – putting Dens and Tannadice among the easiest grounds to spot and navigate to from afar in all of Scotland.

Dundee had its own football lighthouses to guide in travellers from the darkness.

■ A 3pm kick-off at Pittodrie, but it gets dark early in Aberdeen so the lights are on. This was December 5th, 1970. Joey Harper celebrates one of his two goals in a 7-0 rout of Cowdenbeath with his trademark knee-slide.

■ **The first floodlights at St Mirren Park were on very low pylons, which had been purchased from Rangers. The lights had to have a shield fitted on top to prevent them causing confusion to aircraft – the ground was in the flight path of Renfrew Airport. One is shown in the background of this photo of Bobby Carroll, who had been Celtic's first-ever scorer in European competition against Valencia in September 1962. He is training on the snowy Love Street pitch in the fell winter of 1963.**

■ The later, roof-mounted, Love Street lights make a dramatic backdrop to big Jackie Copland about to throw an equally dramatic right hook at Celtic's Icelandic warrior Shuggy Edvaldsson as retribution for what Jackie reckoned had been an overly-robust challenge on his keeper, Ally Hunter. Jackie was, perhaps not surprisingly, ordered off. The final score in the game, on December 17th, 1977, was 3-3.

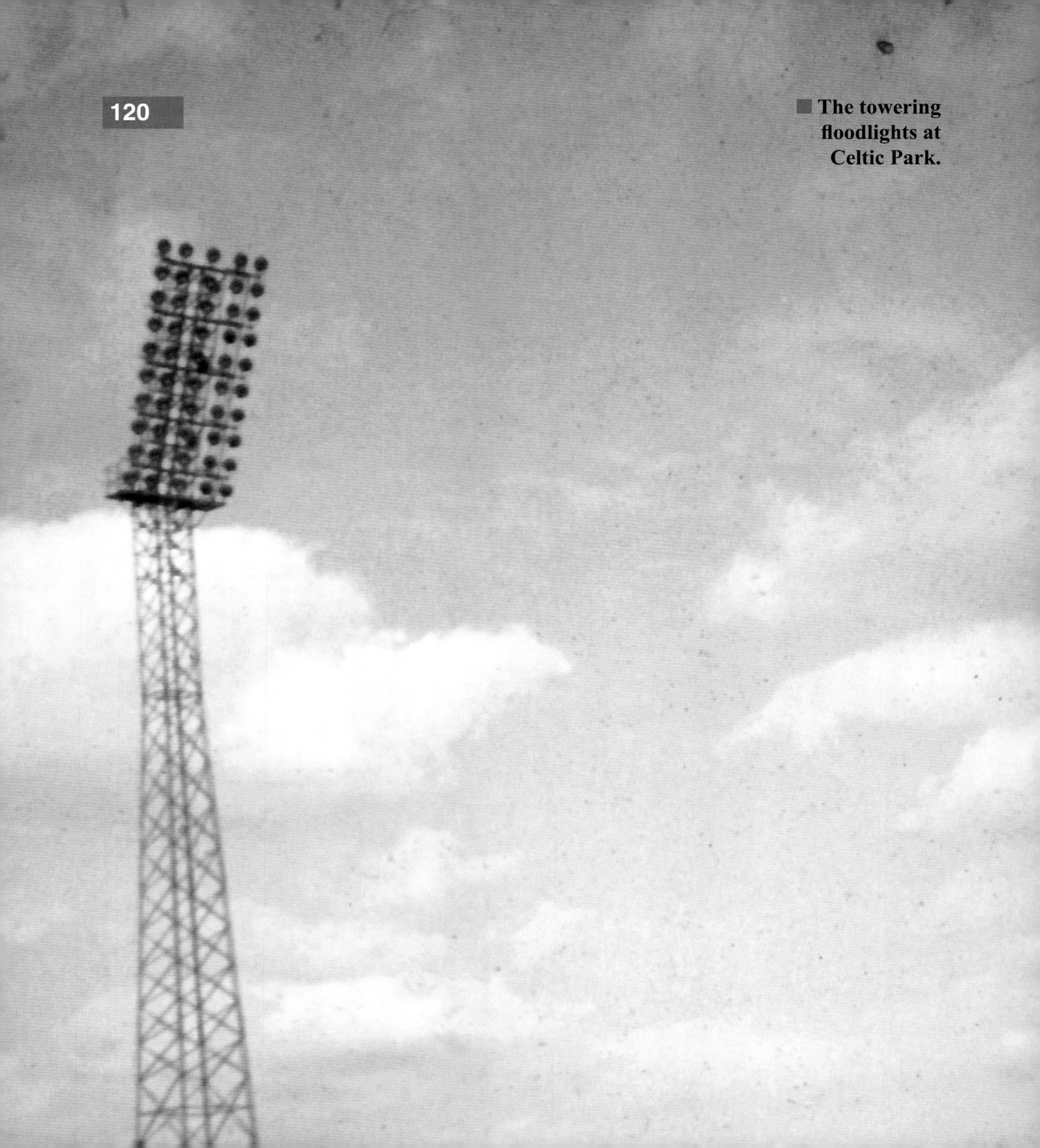

The towering floodlights at Celtic Park.

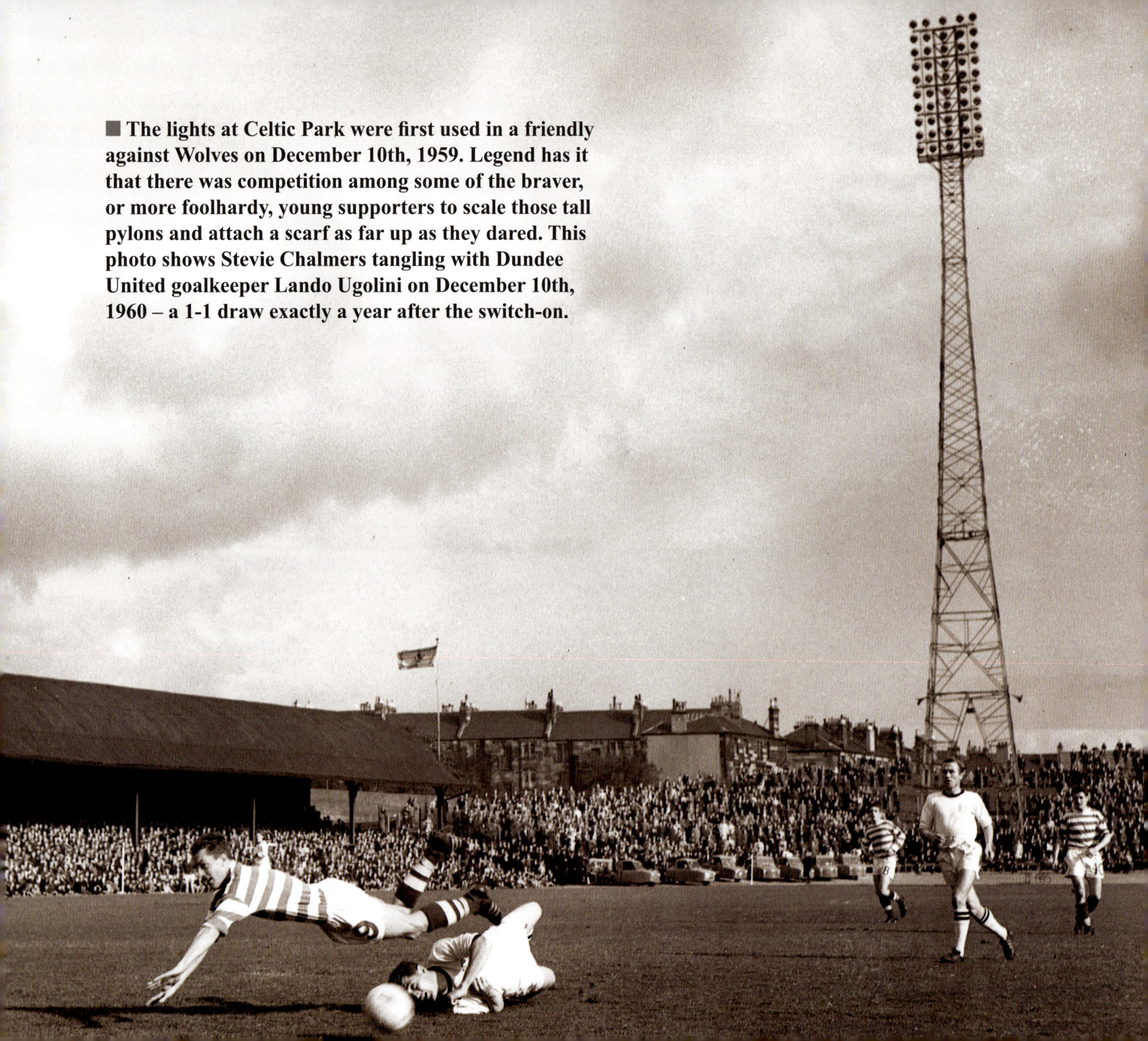

■ **The lights at Celtic Park were first used in a friendly against Wolves on December 10th, 1959. Legend has it that there was competition among some of the braver, or more foolhardy, young supporters to scale those tall pylons and attach a scarf as far up as they dared. This photo shows Stevie Chalmers tangling with Dundee United goalkeeper Lando Ugolini on December 10th, 1960 – a 1-1 draw exactly a year after the switch-on.**

■ **Hibs, with a club tradition of innovation, played under lights in a friendly on Thursday, May 2nd, 1951, at Racing Club de Paris and took note of the positive experience. They also took part in the aforementioned experimental floodlit match at Stenhousemuir, later in 1951. Easter Road's drenchlights went up in the autumn of 1954 and the brightness was the talk of the land. The pylons were stubby, compared to some that would be erected around Scotland, but the quality of the Easter Road lighting shone out for all to see. This was the future. The pic above is from Hibs v Manchester United friendly on Boxing Day 1981. It was a 1-1 draw.**

Greenock Morton's Cappielow is another ground with roof-mounted pylons, although it also has stand-alone pylons.

The Cappielow floodlights were first used in 1958. There was also a friendly against Celtic on February 10th, 1959, which was billed as a "celebration" of the new lights.

At least some of the lamps may have been bought from St Mirren, the ones that had previously been at Ibrox.

This view of the main stand with its roof-mounted pylons is from a bad-tempered Morton v Dunfermline match played on February 22nd, 1969.

The home side had two players sent off before half-time, Joe Mason and Bjarne Jensen, and lost 2-0.

In the early days, some grounds decided their floodlights needed cleaned, from time to time.

At Hampden in 1965, this required brave men to scale the pylons, without safety harnesses or any other specialised equipment, cleaning materials in their pockets, to give the lamps a polish.

The only way to make this climb (once they negotiated the barbed wire crowd control measures shown on the left) was by using short spikes that protruded from the pylon's corner girders.

128

Dates show the first time modern lights were used or installed.

Stenhousemuir	1951
Rangers	1953
Kilmarnock	1953
Falkirk (Brockville)	1953
Hibernian	1954
Partick Thistle	1955
Arbroath	1955
Motherwell	1956
Airdrieonians (Broomfield)	1956
Heart of Midlothian	1957
Dumbarton (Boghead)	1957
Greenock Morton	1958
Queen of the South	1958
Aberdeen	1959
Celtic	1959
St Mirren (Love Street)	1959
Dunfermline Athletic	1959
Dundee	1960
Raith Rovers	1960
Hampden	1961
Stirling Albion (Annfield)	1961
Dundee United	1962
St Johnstone	1964
Clydebank (New Kilbowie)	1965
Cowdenbeath	1968
Albion Rovers	1968
Ayr United	1970
Forfar Athletic	1971
Hamilton Academical (Douglas Park)	1971
Montrose	1971
Berwick Rangers	1972
Brechin City	1977
Alloa Athletic	1979
Stranraer	1981

■ Airdrieonians' Broomfield had pylons on the roof at both sides of the ground,- which leaned over the playing area. The club welcomed Blackburn Rovers to inaugurate the lights on the evening of Monday, October 15th, 1956. This pic shows a Rangers visit on April 22nd, 1972.

■ Every ground looks different under floodlights, and you'll find many supporters who will say their fondest memories of the old days are of their team playing a big game under lights. There was always something more dramatic, more atmospheric, about a floodlit game. If the night sky lends a hand, so much the better. This is Rangers v Dundee on November 13th, 1971. You'll have to take my word for this in a black-and-white photo book but there was a spectacular crimson-and-indigo autumn sunset over Ibrox that evening.

A “classic” pylon at Queen of the South’s Palmerston as Queens draw 1-1 in a First Division encounter with Dundee United on November 30th, 1963. Queens’ lights were first used on October 29th, 1958, in a friendly with Preston North End. The Palmerston pylons are an impressive 80 feet high.

McLEOD'S

■ Floodlights directly behind the goal are unusual in world football but were, conversely, fairly common in Scotland for a couple of decades. Left: December 18th, 1965, Partick Thistle 2, Dundee 0. This shows Firhill's roof-mounted side floodlights plus another set not too far above the crossbar. There were also lights behind the Brockville and Cappielow goals, and those of several other grounds.

■ Above, Davie Wilson scores one of the four goals he got in the Thistle 1, Rangers 4, game of Wednesday, April 17th, 1963 – with another shot of Firhill's behind-the-goal lights in the background.

■ **Falkirk's roof-mounted floodlights were put up in in 1953, inaugurated with a friendly against Newcastle United. They were replaced with a brighter set in 1986.**

This photo shows a visit from Aberdeen (Davie Robb on the ball) on December 25th, 1971. The 1971-72 season was the last that a full set of fixtures took place on Christmas Day, but some matches were still scheduled for December 25th until 1976. Aberdeen won this game 3-0 with two goals from Joey Harper and one from Bertie Miller.

■ Kilmarnock's roof-mounted, tripod-legged lights had a touch of the *War of the Worlds* about them. This is Colin Stein up for a cross during the visit of Rangers on April 24th, 1971. Rangers won 4-1.

■ Right: What better way to show Rugby Park's older lights, hung under the roof of the main stand, than with a photo of Killie's 2-2 draw with Real Madrid in the European Cup on November 17th, 1965. Tommy McLean is shown putting Killie into a 1-0 lead from the penalty spot. Madrid would win the second leg at the Bernabeu 5-1, and went on to capture the trophy for a sixth time. But what a night that was in Kilmarnock!

The lights at Muirton Park were paid for by the St Johnstone Aid Club, a bob-a-week pools competition with 15,000 members which was the brainchild of director Jack McKinlay. They were first used for a game against Hearts on November 28th, 1964. But West Ham United, the FA Cup holders, came to Perth for a special inauguration game on Wednesday, December 16th, 1964.

The Earl of Mansfield held the feu to Muirton Park, although ownership had been gifted to the club by his grandfather on the understanding the land be used only for football and other recreational purposes.

His consent was required for the sale of the ground to Asda, which would in turn lead to the building of McDiarmid Park. The floodlights, then only 25 years old, were to be taken to the new ground to be re-erected.

However, the Earl was concerned that they might be seen, when illuminated, from the windows of Scone Palace.

Balloons were raised to the appropriate height as a test, and the floodlights were shortened by several feet.

As a result, the Earl raised no objections to the club's switch from Muirton to McDiarmid.

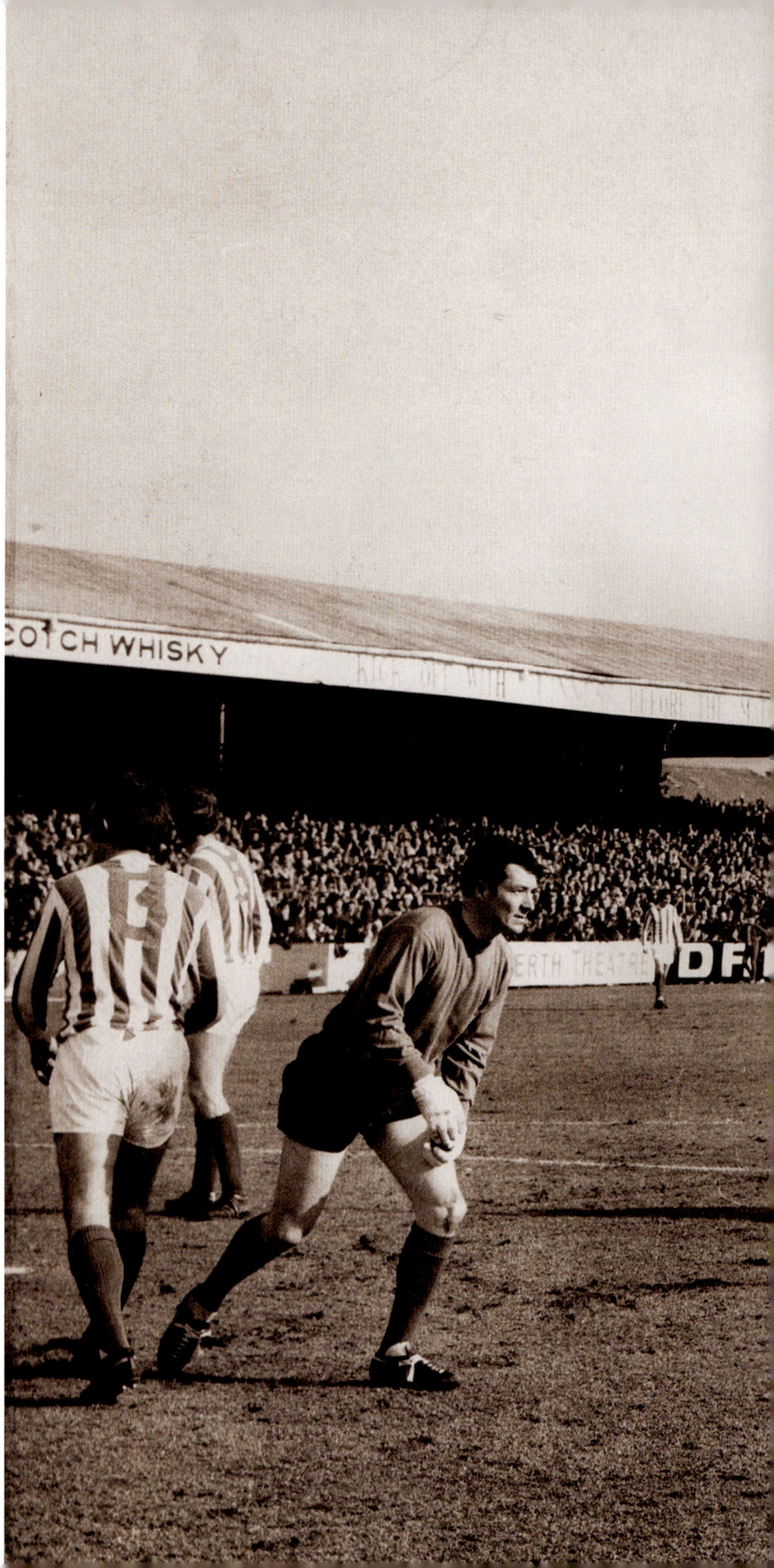

■ **Muirton's lights, but this isn't a St Johnstone game. It is the Scottish Cup Semi-Final of March 14th, 1970, with Aberdeen's Derek "Cup Tie" McKay (No. 7) scoring against Kilmarnock. McKay scored in the Quarter, Semi, and twice in the 3-1 win over Celtic in the Final. The only goals he got for Aberdeen in a brief 16-game career. He had previously played 12 games for Dundee, scoring once. Derek later went to Crystal Palace, though never played in their first team. He had stints at Barrow FC, Elgin City and Buckie Thistle before emigrating to Australia. He died in 2008 but remains a Pittodrie legend.**

PLAYHOUSE
AT MURRAY STREET

Brechin City

IN the ceaseless fight for survival going back to 1906, Brechin City's Glebe Park has seen some tough times. But Brechin proudly keep battling on.

The club moved to Glebe Park in 1919 and the most that ever crammed in was 54 years later when Aberdeen came to play a Scottish Cup tie on February 3rd, 1973.

The crowd of 8,123 saw a highly entertaining 4-2 win for the visitors, inspired by Hungarian star Zoltan Varga.

But the home side certainly didn't disgrace themselves, scoring two late goals and might have given the Dons a real scare if the game had gone on much longer.

The Brechin star on the day was young inside-forward Dave Cunningham who went on to have a lengthy career down south.

This photo is from the early 1950s and shows the old stand, which was replaced in 1981. The low building beside it housed the dressing rooms and offices, and Brechin dignitaries would often watch the game from the veranda in front of it.

6

Queen of the South

NEVER let anyone tell you The Scottish Borders is rugby-only country, Queens have a long and distinguished history in Dumfries.

The biggest attendance at Palmerston came on February 23rd, 1952, when Queens were an established top division club – as they would be for most of the 1950s. It was 26,552 for a Scottish Cup Third Round tie against Hearts.

Queens were only five places below Hearts in the league at the time and the teams had drawn 1-1 in a thrilling league game seven days earlier, in front of 12,500. The crowd for the cup tie was expected to be big, but it was still a tight squeeze to get so many in.

Though there were a lot from Edinburgh (Hearts have always had a fantastic away support) there was a healthy home crowd too. Indeed, The Doonhamers regularly got big crowds in the '50s – average attendance in 1953-54 was above 10,500.

And Palmerston was, and still is, a good ground.

The Portland Drive End, where the home supporters congregate, is the highest terrace upon which standing is allowed that is left in Scotland.

A fine place to watch football.

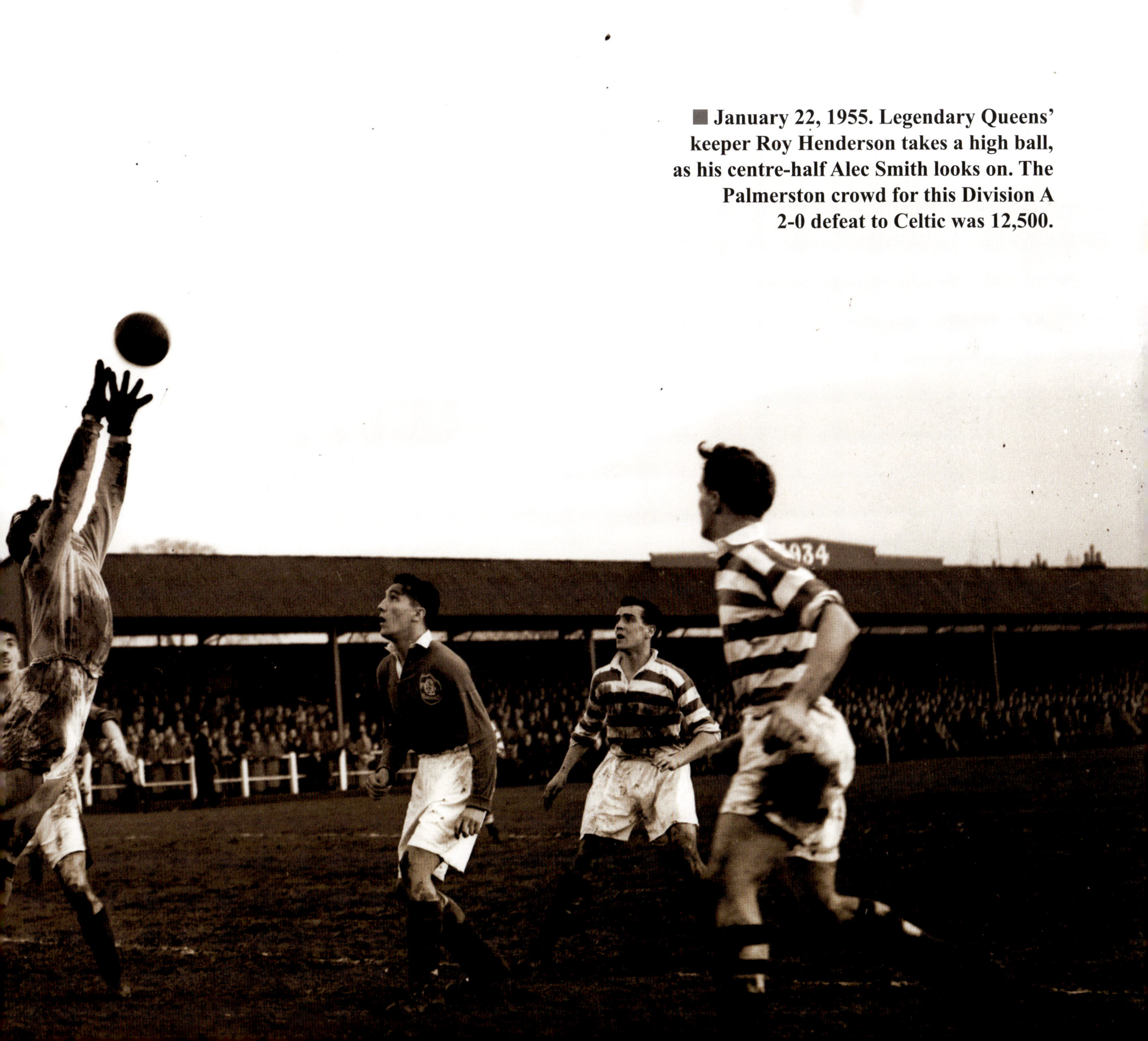

■ January 22, 1955. Legendary Queens' keeper Roy Henderson takes a high ball, as his centre-half Alec Smith looks on. The Palmerston crowd for this Division A 2-0 defeat to Celtic was 12,500.

St Mirren

THE Buddies' best ever crowd should be seen as a massive endorsement of the Scottish League Cup – or at least what the League Cup used to be.

Just after the war, with the Scottish public thirsting for football, the League Cup and its innovative mini-league sections format captured the imagination.

St Mirren had been given a tough draw (which wasn't seeded in those days) in the 1949 competition.

They were in Group 1, along with Celtic, Rangers and Aberdeen.

Things started fairly well for the Saints, they recorded a 3-1 home win over Aberdeen, but followed it with a midweek loss away to Rangers. Celtic came calling on August 20th, 1949, themselves buoyed by a 3-2 win over Rangers then a 5-4 triumph at Pittodrie. St Mirren could leapfrog them if they won, but Celtic were also well placed. It was finely balanced, with all to play for.

And the crowds rolled up to see what would happen.

A total of 47,438 were shoehorned into Love Street, beating the ground's previous record by just 10 more than had seen a St Mirren-Celtic Scottish Cup tie in 1925.

The Saints won 1-0 on that 1949 Saturday afternoon, with a bullet-header from centre-forward Johnny Deakin.

■ Right: this photo was taken on Love Street, March 30th, 1963, as the last few punters get into the Scottish Cup Quarter-Final between Saints and Celtic. The crowd that day was 34,988, giving receipts of £4,944.

ST. MIRREN
FOOTBALL CLUB LTD.
3/ ADMISSION 3/
3/ ADMISSION 3/
3/ ADMISSION 3/

Some of the biggest crowds in Scotland – outwith Glasgow and Edinburgh – have been recorded at Love Street.

The ground held a 40,000-plus crowd as early as 1924 and was still capable of a 42,653 attendance in 1968 for a league match against Rangers.

The newly-promoted club was riding high at the time of that November ’68 game.

Under the inspirational Alex Wright, the Buddies were Britain’s only unbeaten team and second in the league to Jock Stein’s Celtic, fresh from their European Cup triumph.

Wright’s men performed superbly on that frosty day, seeing off Rangers 1-0 with a crisp strike from winger Hugh Gilshan, following a flowing move involving Bobby Pinkerton and Bobby Adamson, midway through the second half.

However, it is the League Cup tie described on the previous page that holds the non-Glasgow or Edinburgh Scottish record crowd.

Quite apart from cup-ties, which set records for many clubs, Love Street also hosted crowds above 40,000 for league games on four occasions.

St Mirren have now moved to a new purpose-built, 8,000-capacity St Mirren Park. The last game at the old ground was a 0-0 draw with Motherwell on January 3rd, 2009.

■ **As on the previous page, this pic is the Scottish Cup Quarter-Final with Celtic of March 30th, 1963. Dick Beattie saves a Stevie Chalmers shot in front of a busy North Bank.**

SCOTTISH DAILY EXPRE S
PIPER
EXTRA EXPORT
makes you feel famous!
PIPER
EXTRA EXPORT

■ Scotland's preparation for the Auld Enemy clash of 1964. From left: Davie Wilson, Denis Law and Alex Hamilton. It was the running track shape that allowed such big crowds to squeeze into Love Street. Those semi-circles behind the goal, added to the terrace around one of the largest playing surfaces in Scotland, gave extra room compared to more squared-off grounds. The dimensions of that playing surface were close to the size of Hampden, allowing players to get a "feel" for what they were about to play on.

■ The terracing at Love Street was a good example of the innovative, sometimes opportunistic, methods of creating steps to stand upon to watch football on top of a rubble base. Earth, bricks, stones and excess building material was dumped, then (starting in 1911) the club paid 6d each for old railway sleepers to create the steps. This photo is from 1984 and shows some very old, but some newer, terrace steps.

■ Left: Icelandic striker Therolf (always known in Paisley as Tottie) Beck training at Love Street in 1963.

The Blond Bombshell was a huge hit with the Buddies, but his career faltered after a move to Ibrox in 1964, where he hardly played a game.

■ Right: Police attempt to calm the raging souls on the North Bank during a highly-charged encounter with Rangers in January 1978.

The main stand on the south side of Love Street was a proper old Scottish football stand. It was completed in 1921 after a prolonged, and stop-start, period of almost 10 years from when work began.

It was a single-tier structure with 1,774 seats, affording a good view of the action, albeit with pillars in the way.

Its length was just 60 yards, centred on the pitch, though the idea was to have it eventually run the full length with sections added when and if they could be afforded. But this never came to pass.

To the left of the stand (as you look at it here, but just out of shot) was the famed Cairter's Corner where Paisley carters and horsemen would stand. It wasn't a place for the faint of heart – these lads called it as they saw it.

The paddock in front of the stand was eventually converted to seating

The original plans for Love Street had set a lofty ambition of a 60,000 capacity – an idea born in the boom-era of football attendances between the world wars. Though never actually achieved, it does indicate the potential of the club.

■ St Mirren v Falkirk, July 26th, 1980, with the stand behind. It was a 2-1 win for The Buddies on their way to the final of the last ever Drybrough Cup.

■ **Above: Robert Hamilton takes a corner in 1954 with the (possibly encouraging, possibly not) shouts of Cairter's Corner behind him. Right: St Mirren v Hibs in 1956, with Saints' Arthur Milne ready to pounce in the unlikely event of any spill that might come from Hibs' Scotland keeper Tommy Younger.**

■ 1958. Saints Keeper Jim Lornie challenges Hearts' Alex Young, closely watched by Archie Buchanan, with Love Street's new North Bank roof being erected in the background.

■ Jim Lornie again, this time shepherding a shot round his post.

Big Jim spent all of his career at Love Street, playing in the 1955 League Cup Final.

After his playing days ended, however, he returned to his North East roots and became Liverpool boss Bill Shankly's talent scout in the Aberdeen area.

The tenements of the royally-named Victoria Street and Albert Street can still be seen (just) in this photo.

Some of the tenements suffered from damp, possibly due to rainwater run-off from the North Bank, and they were eventually demolished.

EVENING DISPATCH

Heart of Midlothian

THE old Tynecastle was one of the great Scottish football stadiums – and it had to be. Hearts have been, over the decades, the third-best supported team in the country behind Glasgow's big two.

■ **This is the 1955 League Cup Quarter-Final second leg. Freddie Glidden jousts with Aberdeen's Paddy Buckley. The other Hearts men in the photo are John Cumming and Bobby Kirk.**

Tynecastle near-disaster of 1932

THERE is an almost-forgotten story behind the biggest crowd ever to attend a game at Tynecastle. Indeed it seems to be mere luck that there wasn't a disaster matching any in the history of Scottish football.

A quite incredible 53,396 attended the Scottish Cup Third Round tie between Hearts and Rangers on February 13th, 1932.

It was one of those ties that had caught the football public's attention. Both clubs knew the Scottish Cup was their best chance of a trophy. Rangers would be runners-up to a superb Motherwell in the league that season, while Hearts (the inter-war years weren't their best period) would finish eighth. But for this game, both sets of supporters had high hopes.

The story can be told in newspaper cuttings of the time. To a modern eye the accounts are at times strange, and yet everyone who ever attended a big game over the years will recognise elements that barely changed in all the years of standing terraces.

This first is from the Edinburgh Evening News, which would have been printed in early afternoon, before the game kicked off, under the heading "A rush to Edinburgh":

The first of the special trains arrived in Edinburgh in the early forenoon, and from shortly after ten o'clock until near the time of the start there was a steady procession of trains to both the Waverley and Princes Street stations.

No fewer than 16 specials came from Glasgow and district; and the Borders, North Berwick, and Bathgate also sent contingents.

From Fifeshire five special trains arrived at Waverley Station, while to both stations' local services were considerably augmented.

Large numbers of charabancs and motors also arrived in the city during the forenoon and other types of vehicles came from the West carrying supporters of the Ibrox club.

In Princes Street a large number of members of one of the "brake clubs" paraded the thoroughfare wearing blue berets and blue scarves. They were on the whole well behaved, although very enthusiastic.

It was estimated by the railway authorities that nearly 20,000 visitors entered Edinburgh for the big tie.

"Brake clubs" were organisations that would travel to away games.

The accounts of "very enthusiastic" parades of supporters through Princes Street will be familiar to all who attended games in the 1960s and '70s.

This next report tells of the scene at the ground:

The first arrivals were a band of enthusiasts who took up their position shortly after eight o'clock this morning awaiting the opening of the gates at 12.30. The queue lengthened as time went on, and an hour and a half before the game was due to start the four-shilling stand accommodation was fully taken up.

By that time, too, there would be nearly 20,000 inside the ground, and three-quarters of an hour later that figure

bad been doubled. And there were thousands outside the ground awaiting admission. It seemed probable that the record for Tynecastle of 51,000-odd would be broken.

The police acted as stewards. Constables were in front of several areas, marshalling the crowd closer together, and the arrangements worked in fairly convincing fashion.

The crowd was on the whole fairly quiet, even the Rangers supporters, conspicuous by their blue favours, being slow to begin their customary choruses.

When they did, it was in earnest. The songs were prefaced by an outburst of cheering – cheering which was promptly "drowned" by the radio-gramophone apparatus which had been giving musical selections since 12.30.

Meantime the parking went on, but it was noticeable there were several areas where the crowd were slow to gather. The police at this stage had a fairly hard task; the stumbling-block in an area being a "camp" of Rangers supporters, complete with flags and banners, and wearing the inevitable blue berets and scarves. In other spots could be seen several in maroon hats and scarves – the opposing "camps" – a fair distance, however, from each other.

The appearance of Mr W. Struth, the Rangers manager, was the signal for a cheer from the Ibrox enthusiasts, and then attention was again turned to the attempt to get the crowd to fill up the more roomy areas.

The first signal to the ambulance men came at half-past two, and by that time the crowds in the looser packed areas were getting together. The police were succeeding.

Meantime the ambulance corps were getting busier, the long wait and the crowding taking their toll.

At this point it was quite benign. Just a big crowd on a big day. Some of the detail, such as the police herding crowds closer together to fit more in, look unusual, perhaps amusing, to a modern eye.

Later reports tell of the situation that transpired as the game went on. This article is from the Aberdeen Press & Journal, published the Monday after the game:

There were sensational scenes at Tynecastle where a record crowd numbering 55,000 saw Rangers oust Hearts by the only goal of the game.

Behind both goals the terracing held swaying humanity, packed tightly together, and as the ball swept from one end of the field to the other the dense crowd, in their eagerness not to miss the run of the ball, swayed dangerously.

Latterly, one of the crush barriers at the Gorgie Road End gave way under the terrific strain, and thousands of spectators lurched forward, falling to the foot of the embankment.

The utmost alarm prevailed for two or three minutes and handkerchiefs were waved by the dozen, summoning the stretcher men.

In the wild surging forward a number of onlookers, including women, were knocked down and trampled on, while others collapsed through severe crushing.

The remarkable thing is that in the wild scramble no one was seriously injured. From the stands it appeared certain that serious physical damage had been caused to many of the hemmed-in spectators. Two men were taken to the Royal Infirmary, but were allowed home.

Waving of handkerchiefs was the accepted way of summoning medical help in those days, a tradition that persisted in Scottish football, and among other types of crowds, until the advent of mobile phones.

This "lurch forward", piling people on top of each other, clearly came close to a very serious situation. Every reader who was ever at a football game in the black and white era will recognise what it was like to be in a crowd like this.

It's a wonder any of us survived!

■ This photo shows Tynecastle with just a shade less than 25,000 – not even half the 1932 record attendance discussed on the previous page.

Alan Anderson tackles former Hearts man Willie Wallace. Roy Kay is the Hearts player in the background, with Celtic's Tommy Callaghan on the right.

It is a 1-1 League draw on February 27th, 1971 – Eric Carruthers for Hearts, Harry Hood for Celtic.

The main stand, with its paddock in front, was an Archibald Leitch design, and held 4,000. Construction on the stand started in 1914, but it wasn't completed until after the end of World War 1.

It was demolished in 2017.

WORLD WIDE TRAVEL
NATION WIDE CAR HIRE
MACKAY BROS
ESSO... BUY ESSO
DRIVE ESSO
MACKINLAY'S
REMINGTON

This is one of the most famous goals in Scottish football history.

It is March 29th, 1958, Hearts against Raith Rovers at Tynecastle.

Jimmy Wardhaugh heads Hearts' 120th First Division goal of the season to surpass the 119 Motherwell had scored in season 1931-32.

Hearts would go on to set a new Scottish top-flight record of 132 goals as they won the 1957-58 Championship. It is a total that has never been passed since.

It was also the only time a Scottish top-flight team scored over 100 goals (103, to be precise) more than they conceded in a season.

If you took a poll of opposition teams' fans to ask which was their favourite "away" trip, a high proportion would say Tynecastle.

The canyon-like streets of tenements surrounding the stadium made it a delight to "find" for supporters coming off trains or buses.

It was especially exciting to glimpse the floodlights (though this game v Motherwell is from the era before floodlights) for a night game, shining above the roofs and leading fans towards it for a night game.

Though it didn't have the highest terraces, or much cover against the elements, the ground always generated a fantastic atmosphere.

This game was December 8th, 1956. Hearts won 3-2. In the photo are Bobby Kirk (No.2), Jimmy Milne (No.5) and Tom McKenzie is guarding the goal line. The goalkeeper is Gordon Marshall at the start of his distinguished Hearts career.

The crowd was 35,000.

■ Tynecastle at its most memorable for a generation of fans. August 31st, 1985. Sandy Clark has just scored a late derby winner and the Wheatfield corner goes berserk.

■ **The mid-terrace, entry was quite rare in Scottish football stadium design.**

More usual was the requirement for supporters to walk up paths or stairs on the outer perimeter slope and enter the ground over the brim. Mid-level entries were, however, common in grandstands.

This entry at Tynecastle's Gorgie End was built in the 1920s.

Ibrox, Celtic Park, Hampden and Rugby Park also had such entrances, but they were rare because they reduced terracing space. They were used only as a necessity when terraces were hemmed in by surrounding buildings or other encroaching geographical features.

The Gorgie End of Tynecastle was tight against the tenements behind.

This is Hearts v Rangers on October 10th, 1978.

February 1970. Hearts assistant manager Jock Wallace supervises winger Drew Young in what looks like a very punchy training session. Aye, Jock was tough! Hearts would often use Tynecastle as a fitness training venue.

■ **Ian Crawford, the 1956 Hearts Scottish Cup Final hero (wearing a style of strip and collar that remains much loved by Hearts fans) with the Tynecastle main stand behind.**

What's this? Legendary Hibs keeper Tommy Younger in a Hearts strip at Tynecastle?

It is, however, an Edinburgh Select playing Bolton Wanderers on August 7th, 1954, in front of a 45,000 crowd.

This was the annual Charities Cup match between an Edinburgh Select and a top-flight English side before the domestic season started. The SFA, before 1966, didn't sanction pre-season friendlies unless they were charity games.

These matches took place between 1944 and 1962. If the game was at Tynecastle there would be six Hearts players and five from Hibs playing in Hearts' home colours, and it would be the other way round for games at Easter Road. Strictly speaking, Leith Athletic and Edinburgh City players could also have been selected.

The Edinburgh players in this photo are, from left: John Cumming (Hearts), Jimmy Wardhaugh (Hearts), Bobby Combe (Hibs), and Tommy Younger (Hibs).

Edinburgh beat Bolton 3-2 after being 2-0 down at half-time. This photo shows Harry Hassall (who played in the celebrated 1953 FA Cup Final) getting one of the Wanderers' goals. The great Nat Lofthouse got the other, though some reports at the time harshly credited Freddie Glidden with an o.g. – he couldn't have got out of the way if he'd tried!

The Edinburgh scorers were Alfie Conn (47 min.), Jimmy Wardhaugh (72 min), and Gordon Smith (80 min.).

■ The great Jimmy Wardhaugh, with another view of the old Tynecastle stand in the background. This was a 2-1 win for Hearts over Dundee, on October 17th, 1953. Jimmy was one of the Gorgie scorers that day, along with Alfie Conn. The Dark Blues' keeper Bobby Henderson is gathering the ball, with South African full-back Gordon Frew alongside.

Tunnels

FOOTBALL grounds have their quirks. And in the old days, before all grandstands were made to the same pattern, they had even more quirks. The tunnel was one of these.

It is, of course, one of the most basic functions of a ground. There has to be a way for the players to get to the field.

This was an important part of the ritual. A couple of minutes before 3pm, all eyes turned to the tunnel. In the days before fanfares blared from the PA system, the clue the players were about to emerge was that the ball-boys scurried out first.

A roar went up. Expectations were high, nerves were tested. Every player remembers the moment he walked out of a tunnel to make his debut in front of a crowd as a pro footballer.

Some grounds had steps or ramps down to the pitch, some entrances were on the level, a few had steps up to the playing area. Some tunnels were right on the half-way line, some were in corners. It depended on the architecture of the main stand, and sometimes the lie of the land surrounding it.

Sometimes, the players were very close to the fans as they walked out – this was long before anyone thought of extendable plastic sleeves that stretch out to give cover.

But, of course, some grounds didn't have tunnels at all. There is absolutely nothing consistent about Scottish football grounds!

■ **Left: Alex Ferguson running out the Ibrox tunnel on a frosty day in February 1968.**

■ **Right: George Best emerges from the Easter Road tunnel for his Hibs home debut, v Partick Thistle, on December 1st, 1979. The crowd was 20,622 – more than quadruple Hibs' last home gate against Thistle on April 28th that year.**

Bukta

■ With the biggest, grandest stand in the land, the tunnel at Ibrox, right on the centre line of the pitch, was the most impressive in Scotland.

It was easily wide enough for both teams to come out at once (although this didn't happen for every game) and was a level walk starting deep inside the stand.

This photo shows a sombre affair, unlike most other match days.

Rangers captain John Greig and Dundee United skipper Doug Smith lead their sides on to the field on January 16th, 1971.

It was two weeks after the Ibrox Disaster, Rangers' first game since it happened.

A minute's silence was observed for the dead.

■ Celtic Park's old tunnel and railed-off area, saw several changes over the years, and then a wholesale revamp in the 1971 stand rebuild. Above: August 5th, 1969, a friendly between the Scottish and English league champions of 1968-69, Celtic and Leeds United. Billy Bremner and Billy McNeill lead their teams out, closely examining their boots. The game was a 1-1 draw in front of 65,000.

■ Celtic Park's new, wider tunnel area on September 8th, 1973. Clyde's players applaud Celtic on to the park, marking the unfurling of the home side's eighth championship flag in a row. The SFA allowed Celtic to have every player wear a No. 8 on their shorts to mark the occasion. If the Celtic players were grateful for Clyde's sporting respect, they didn't show it in a 5-0 win that included a Bobby Lennox hat-trick and a very rare thing – a Danny McGrain goal after a smart one-two with Jimmy Johnstone.

■ **Until about 100 years ago, most grounds had pavilions which didn't really lend themselves to the provision of a tunnel. The pavilion at Airdrieonians' Broomfield, shown here, stayed in place longer than that of any other club. Players merely walked down its steps to the pitch. This is 1958, with Airdrie's young man-mountain centre-half Doug Baillie leading his team out.**

■ **Another pavilion, Tannadice before the cantilevered stand was built (see Volume 2). This is Dunfermline captain Ron Mailer on Saturday, April 29th, 1961, showing off the Scottish Cup that The Pars had taken in a replayed final v Celtic the previous Wednesday (the Cup Final was rarely the last game of the season in those days). There were a few steps up from the pavilion at the corner of United's ground.**

■ **There wasn't a tunnel at Dens Park either. The players came out a door then ran down a paved ramp (more difficult when aluminium studs were introduced). This photo shows Jim McLean making his debut for Dundee on September 11th, 1965. However, the team he would manage with such success, Dundee United from across the road, won 5-0 that day. The players behind Jim are Charlie Cooke and Kenny Cameron.**

■ Left: The narrow Rugby Park tunnel (with Davie Cooper emerging from it in November 1982) had a claustrophobic, prison-like feel to it.

■ Above: Ayr's Somerset Park tunnel in 1959, with trainer Eddie Summers practising his running-on-with-magic-sponge technique. Although it looks more like a magic tea-towel.

■ Left: Hampden, despite being the mightiest stadium in the Northern Hemisphere for around 80 years, had a very plain, almost apologetic gap under the stand serving as the entry-point to the arena. It didn't really merit the title "tunnel".

Picture shows Scotland and Northern Ireland captains George Young and Danny Blanchflower leading out their teams for the November 3rd, 1954, Home International. It was a 2-2 draw.

The dapper gent sitting beside the dugout is the (by then) former Rangers manager Mr Bill Struth.

■ Right: Partick Thistle's Firhill had a similarly understated entry to the playing area. A door, a few steps, and that was it.

This photo shows two Thistle legends, goalkeeper Tommy Ledgerwood and full-back Jimmy McGowan, in 1953.

■ **Third Lanark's Ally MacLeod comes out of the Cathkin Park pavilion in 1954 (though, like other pavilions, it isn't a tunnel as such) with an admiring young lad.**

■ **Celtic legend Bertie Peacock leads his team out of the Brockville tunnel on January 28th, 1961, past a policeman who is wearing an early-model walkie-talkie radio . . . or is one of the Cybermen from *Dr Who*.**

■ **At Clyde's Shawfield, the players emerged from the tunnel out of the stand, down a few steps, a walkway over the dog racing track, then passed through a gate to get on to the pitch. This photo was taken at the Clyde v Aberdeen game of December 14th, 1974, and reveals Freddie Mercury's brief career as a Don!**

■ This was one of the odder Scottish football ground tunnel quirks.

Motherwell struck a sponsorship deal with a Glasgow carpet shop for this game – the photo is from February 28th, 1976, a 1-0 win for Rangers.

As an advertising ploy, the teams ran out over a carpet sample rolled out at the end of the Fir Park tunnel.

It isn't known how many supporters in the 25,241 crowd thought: "Ooh, my favourite player is running over a carpet with a bonny swirly pattern and a colour that perfectly matches my wally dugs. It would look just right in my front room."

This was when scruffy old balls were used for the pre-game kickabout (now known as a warm-up and organised to a quite incredible degree compared to the informal scenes of old).

Ross County

THE rise of County is one of the great success stories of Scottish football.

Their journey from Highland League to the very top of the tree, bypassing and outstripping several long-established League clubs on the way, is a model of good management and good organisation behind the scenes.

The administration supporting such sustained growth will have been every bit as important as good play on the pitch because it certainly isn't easy to become a Scottish Premier club.

Victoria Park has had to change too. It was little more than Junior-standard when County were in the Highland League. The toilets in the corner had soakaway drains (no drains at all, in other words) and could be quite pungent.

The biggest crowd (of 8,500) was for a Scottish Cup tie against Rangers in 1966.

The transition to a modern ground was achieved through investment, hard work – and was forged in fire!

■ **This photo, from 1969, shows grass banks instead of terraces and a few rows of undercover terracing behind the Jail End goal. County finished third in the 1968-69 Highland League table, behind Inverness Thistle and champions Elgin City.**

196

■ Victoria Park, 1966. The club replaced this wooden stand in early 1990, and built a new one. But how did they get rid of the old stand? See next page.

County didn't demolish their old stand, or even attempt to deconstruct it. They left it where it was and in April 1990 set it on fire!

They were able to do this because Victoria Park football ground is set within Jubilee Park in Dingwall. All the same, the blaze sent a pall of black smoke floating over the town.

A sizeable crowd of County supporters and club dignitaries gathered on the pitch to watch the entertainment. There were also a good number of firefighters to keep an eye on proceedings.

The old wooden stand had been in place since 1927 but was sagging into dilapidation and had come to be considered inadequate for the modern game. It didn't match County's ambitions.

However, no matter the inadequacies the stand had as a place to watch football, it certainly burned very well, becoming quite the roaring inferno within minutes of a match being put to it.

Work began on the replacement, with its cantilevered roof, almost as soon as the embers of the old one had cooled. It cost £250,000 and seated 300. It is now known as the West Stand.

■ **Right: firefighters stand by in case they are needed at the 1990 controlled burning of the old stand.**

Clydebank

IT was an eventful but ultimately tragic life for Clydebank who played their home games at New Kilbowie Park.

The ground's two record crowds were in February 1965, only two days apart, when they were playing under the title of E. S. Clydebank (the merged name with East Stirlingshire).

Sunderland visited to inaugurate the ground's floodlights, which director Jack Steedman colourfully claimed were "the best in Britain". Sunderland won 5-1, with Steedman's nephew, and future Scotland manager, Andy Roxburgh getting the home goal.

Then they played a Scottish Cup First Round replay against Hibernian, the clubs having drawn 1-1 at Easter Road four days previously. The first cup tie was played on the Saturday, the Sunderland game was on the Monday, then the replay took place on the Wednesday. Hibs won it 2-0.

The Sunderland match drew a 10,000 crowd, while the cup replay was seen by 11,500 (though some sources give a 14,900 attendance, this was probably a boastful claim).

By the mid 1970s it seemed a new football power was rising. The club achieved promotion to the Premier Division in 1977, as runners-up to Alex Ferguson's St Mirren.

Davie Cooper would be transferred to Rangers for £100,000, putting the club on a firmer financial footing, and bench seats were installed all round the ground. These were heady times for New Kilbowie.

That first sojourn in the top division lasted just one season, though they did get up again for a further two seasons.

It all ended badly, though. The ground was sold in 1996 and the club suffered a nomadic existence at Cappielow and Boghead for the next six years.

There was a short-lived (and very unpopular) plan to relocate the operation to Dublin, but still play in the Scottish leagues. There were also suggestions that the club might bring Scottish league football to Galashiels or even Carlisle. But while these ideas might have been ambitious and innovative, they came to nothing.

The death knell came in 2002 when the club fell into administration. Its few remaining assets (mainly membership of the SFL and SFA) were bought by Airdrie United and the Clydebank name died.

There is a stark warning in the tale of Clydebank's last few years. It is simply this: whatever happens, try not to lose ownership of your ground. Clubs who don't own their ground will almost inevitably be blown on to the rocks by the unforgiving winds of cold economics.

■ **Scotland played Wales in an amateur youth international at New Kilbowie on April 3rd, 1965. Scotland won 3-0, with one of the goals scored by Alex MacDonald who would go on to be a St Johnstone and Rangers star. Another scorer was Ian Waddell, then a Queen's Park player who later played for Airdrie, Hamilton and East Stirling. Others in the team included: goalkeeper Jim Eadie (Balloch Juveniles) who had a long career in the English Leagues; Ian Sneddon of Drumchapel Amateurs who played for Hearts and Morton; Billy McAlpine of Gorgie Hearts who signed for Hearts; George Cumming of Motherwell Bridge Works who played for Partick, then became a referee and worked for UEFA in referee management; and Arthur Duncan of Falkirk High School who became a full international while with Hibs.**

■ **You can make up your own mind on the wisdom, or otherwise, of bench seats on uncovered terracing to watch a winter sport in Scotland. In truth, the club had little choice. The rules for Scottish stadiums at the time dictated 10,000 seats had to be in place to play in the top league. However, it is also true that installation of seats allowed the capacity of the crowd to fall just below 10,000, thus avoiding the consequential expenses of**

making it a "designated ground" under the new Criminal Justice (Scotland) Act. The perverse – perhaps it might be described as cruel – attitude of Clydebank polis in the 1980s and '90s should also be mentioned. No matter what the weather was like, or how many (or how few) supporters were in attendance, they insisted you sit down and remain sitting. If this meant you sat in a puddle during a deluge, tough!

Stirling Albion

THE record crowd at Stirling Albion's old Annfield ground was a very impressive 28,600. It is even more impressive when you learn it was an all-ticket game, and only 28,000 tickets had been sold.

The date was March 14th, 1959, a Scottish Cup quarter-final against Celtic. Albion were a First Division club at the time, in the middle of their yo-yo years.

The club was promoted to Scotland's top division in 1949, 1951, 1953, 1958, 1961 and 1965, but relegated in 1950, 1952, 1956, 1960, 1962 and 1968. They haven't been in the top division since.

As was common in those days, no one really knew why there were so many at the game, or how at least 600 more supporters than the capacity figure were allowed in.

It was, however, extremely dangerous. A wall between the stand and terracing collapsed, sending fans leaping on to the track to avoid being crushed. They stayed by the side of the pitch for the rest of the game.

Newspapers, with their airy 1950s disregard for safety, described it as: "Fans perched here, fans perched there. Fans everywhere but on the net strings." Celtic won 3-1.

■ This photo show Hearts' Jimmy Wardhaugh attempting a looping header in a League Cup sectional game at Annfield on Saturday, August 15th, 1959. The crowd that day was a mere 11,117. Hearts won 2-1.

■ A crowd of 12,000 saw Rovers give a good account of themselves before going down 2-0 to Rangers in a Drybrough Cup Quarter-Final on July 27th, 1974.

KEG HEAVY

■ **Annfield was built in 1945 in the grounds of Annfield House, an 18th Century mansion that had fallen on hard times. It can be seen behind the terrace roof in this photo. The club used it for offices and dressing rooms until the 1970s. There was a narrow, walled-off path for players to reach the pitch. With Albion moving to Forthbank in 1992, Annfield House is now a care home. What was once the pitch has become a leafy residential area. This photo shows Rangers' John Prentice attempting to chip Albion keeper Bill Robertson in a 2-2 draw on October 22nd, 1955.**

Dunfermline Athletic

DUNFERMLINE'S slide from their former status as one of the nation's most successful clubs, regularly winning trophies and possessing a fine European pedigree, is one of the saddest stories in Scottish football.

This is (by a whisker) the largest town in Fife, and the 11th biggest town in the country – more populous than Motherwell, Perth, Kilmarnock or Inverness. If The Pars punched their weight, they would always be a top-flight club.

It is a sleeping giant.

East End Park was, in the 1960s and 70s, a great ground. The L-shaped cover on the north and west terracing generated a very good atmosphere.

The biggest-ever crowd is recorded as 27,160, when champions Celtic visited the cup-winners in 1968. Though that is the official figure, hundreds, possibly thousands, more had gained entrance that April night.

The capacity of East End Park has shrunk drastically with the all-seater era, but the main stand, now known as The South Stand, backing on to the Halbeath Road, retains its character and still gives the place much of its personality.

■ **Right: Eric Martin clutches the ball at the feet of Joe McBride (with the South Stand in the background) on November 20th, 1966. It was one of the best games ever seen at the ground, though The Pars lost 5-4 to Celtic after three times being two goals ahead. Kick-off was delayed to let the 22,000 crowd in.**

212

■ **Above: a proper Scottish football ground: East End Park in the mid 1960s. The new 1962 stand is on the left. The north and west shed roofs were joined to make the distinctive L-shape in 1967.**

■ **Left: Jock Stein with most of his 1961 Scottish Cup-winning side in front of the old stand. It was built not long after World War 1 and bore some resemblance to the old stand at Tannadice (see Volume 2 of this book). The stand had been slightly upgraded when the club bought 2,500 seats – 800 of them "tip-ups" – at a sale of Dunfermline Ice Rink's furnishings in September 1955.**

The line-up is, back, from left: Willie Cunningham, Cammie Fraser, Eddie Connachan, Ron Mailer, Jackie Williamson, George Miller. Front: Jock Stein, Tommy McDonald, Alex Smith, Charlie Dickson, George Peebles, Harry Melrose, and trainer Jimmy Stevenson.

■ **October 12th, 1974.**

The Pars' giant Norwegian keeper Geir Karlsen looks like he might have let this effort from Rangers' Derek Parlane go past him.

However, the photo gives a decent view of the long shed roof over East End Park's north side.

The roof extended round behind the far goal.

It was a great place to watch a game of football, and deafening when the native Fifers were in full cry urging their team on.

Younger's TA
LO
Esso
TOP TEAM ROYAL

■ Former Scotland international goalkeeper George Farm and his son have a run-about on the East End Park pitch in August 1968, with the ground's east terracing behind. George had just managed Dunfermline to their second Scottish Cup win of the Sixties. He was quite a player too, having been in goal for Blackpool in the famous "Stanley Matthews final" when the Seasiders won the FA Cup in 1953. He also won promotion to the First Division for Queen of the South and Raith Rovers as a boss.

A grainy photo of the new East End Park stand under construction in 1962, with an exotic (and quite rare) two-tone Austin Metropolitan Fixed-Head Coupe parked outside. A rather less sexy Austin A30 is driving along Halbeath Road.

Partick Thistle

ASIDE from Queen's Park, Thistle are the only other Scottish side whose ground has a highest attendance record for a game they weren't playing in.

On February 25th, 1928, Scotland played Northern Ireland at Firhill in front of 54,723.

The highest home crowd for a Thistle game was 49,838 for a League encounter against Rangers six years earlier on February 18th, 1922. The Jags were Scottish Cup holders at the time. In Scotland, only Celtic, Rangers, Hearts and Hibs have ever recorded higher crowds than that for a League game.

Thistle lost that game 1-0 to a late Alan Morton strike. Just before the goal, Thistle's 'keeper Ken Campbell was badly injured (though he played on) after being crushed against one of the goalposts in a penalty box stramash.

Thistle moved to Firhill in 1909, which was, in its heyday, possibly the archetypal mid-sized Scottish football ground.

A main stand, built in 1927, a large, long covered area opposite to shelter from the elements and where the noise came from, a quirky half-roof on one end, an open terrace at the other, and the freedom to walk round so you could choose which goal you wanted to stand behind.

Not too big (although the original aim was for an 80,000-capacity stadium) but not small. Crush barriers to lean on, a perimeter wall that youngsters sat on (perched eight feet above the greyhound racing track) and proper corners. There were the obligatory roof supports so you had to carefully select where you stood to ensure a clear view of both goals.

It was flanked by gloomy tenements on one side, and Firhill Basin (part of the Forth & Clyde Canal) on the other.

It always smelled like a football ground, and sounded like a football ground. It was dusty and decrepit in places. It had history. You could tell there had been great times but you could also sense the bitter disappointments it had seen. It was a great place to watch football.

The shed roof opposite the main stand was put up in 1954, largely paid for by a couple of good runs in the League Cup.

For many years the main stand had a line of huts along the front. These were betting booths for Firhill's dog racing nights.

■ **Right: Davie Meiklejohn, a Rangers all-time-great player, then a revered manager of Thistle from 1947 until his death in 1959. He is pictured in 1953, Homburg hat and glasses case by his side, in the enclosure in front of the Firhill stand with the tote booths behind.**

"Meek" died in an ambulance after suffering a heart attack at Broomfield. He had been watching from the pavilion as his Partick side played Airdrie in a League Cup sectional game. He was 58.

The two sides of the ground. This page, the main stand, behind one of Thistle's all-time-greats, John MacKenzie, the Firhill Flyer. Opposite: the shed on that huge canal-side terracing.

ORD
JOHN BANKS ORGANISATION
McEWAN'S EXPORT
THE BEST buy in BEER
LONG JOHN
JAMES LONGMUIR & SONS LTD
Rag, Woollen & Metal Merchants
133-141 BROOK ST
S.E. and BRANCHES
Tel. 041.554.8888
things go better with
Coke
DRINK
Coca-Cola
You always know the score if your account is with the ...
JOHN BANKS ORGANISATI
21-23 KELVINGROVE STREET, GLASGOW C.3. Tel. 041.248

■ Thistle's Tommy Ledgerwood dodges round Aberdeen's Jack Dunbar, in the days when shinguards were rather hefty items.

Tommy is trying to get a quick drop-kick away.

One of the reasons goalkeepers used to part with the ball fast was that it was fair play for forwards to barge them in an attempt to get them to drop the ball, or even push them over the line – for which a goal could be given.

This photo shows Firhill on September 6th, 1952, before the canal-side got its roof.

It was a 1-1 Division A draw.

■ **Firhill in 1976. This photo was taken from the City End which had, unusually, two types of crush barriers – some of metal, some of concrete. The terracing has been demolished but not (so far) replaced. There have been various plans for a 1,000-seat, then a 450-seat stand – possibly including flats – but finance and planning issues have held it up. The grass bank there now is ruefully titled "The Bing" by Thistle supporters.**

■ **Firhill was one of those grounds you could see into from outside. Although the figures up on the Nolly Bank at the top of this photo would need very good eyesight to judge whether Paul Wilson is being fouled in this Thistle v Celtic game of October 10th, 1977. Thistle won 1-0 in front of 26,000.**

McGHEE'S BAKERY

The is the view from the terracing behind the north end goal, looking towards Glasgow city centre.

The structure at the far end of the stand was the social club, although this had been badly damaged by a fire in the mid-1970s.

This photo was taken on November 6th, 1982, Thistle are beating St Johnstone 3-1.

The high drop to pitch level came about when the front rows of terracing were removed in 1928 to make room for the greyhound track.

Rangers outside-right Willie McCulloch tries to get a cross past Dave Mathers in December 1953. The Murano Street and Firhill Road tenements are visible in the background.

Down south

THEY also play football, although not very well, south of the Border in England. So we'll take a short tour around some of their stadiums.

Compared to Scotland there are fewer League teams per head of population in England. This means that many large cities, such as Leeds, Leicester, Sunderland, and Newcastle – all with big populations – have only one club.

In theory, this should mean huge stadiums getting huge numbers through the gates, especially in the boom years of the 1930s and 1950s. But while the likes of Roker Park (record attendance 75,118), St James' Park (68,386) and Hillsborough (72,841) saw big crowds, their best aren't close to the big grounds in Scotland.

Similarly, apart from the famous Wembley "white horse" FA Cup Final of 1923, when many thousands gained entry without paying, the national stadium never got anywhere near the gigantic attendance figures that Hampden can boast.

But, to be fair, England has (or had before the all-seater era) some magnificent and truly beautiful football stadiums.

■ **Right: There was a long history of dog racing at Wembley, from 1927 to the late 1990s. There were permanent kennels at the stadium until 1973. The low lights for the dog track obscured the view from the terraces, though, and were usually removed for big football games.**

■ Wembley was opened in 1923, and initially known as The Empire Stadium as one of its purposes was as a centrepiece of the 1925 British Empire Exhibition. Some of the other pavilions for that event are shown in the foreground of this photo. The old stadium was a terrible place to watch football. The terraces behind the goal were so far from the action as to need binoculars, and the gentle slope meant only the exceptionally tall could see everything on the pitch. Mind you, Scots fans didn't usually care. The Tartan Army (not that they were called that in those days) thoroughly enjoyed their Home Internationals trip to London every second year.

■ London's White City Stadium was never a permanent base for a football club, though QPR played there for two seasons in the 1930s and one in the 1960s. The most famous game was a 2-1 win for Uruguay over France in a 1966 World Cup group match that had to be moved from Wembley because there was dog racing scheduled that night. White City was demolished in 1985 but in its day was a sprawling stadium. The running track was 600 yards, compared to the normal 400 metres. Like Wembley, the spectators' view was never good. Built for the 1908 Olympics, this is the stadium which (it is claimed) decided the length of the modern marathon. The 1896 Athens Olympics marathon was 40 km (24.85 miles), while the 1900 Paris Olympics marathon was just over 25 miles. The 1908 race was fixed at 26 miles, 385 yards, because that was the length of the course from under the nursery window at Windsor Castle to the finish line in front of White City's royal box. It has remained that distance, the only non-metric Olympic athletics event.

There are striking similarities, as well as great differences, when stadiums in Scotland and England are compared. The main stand at Sunderland's Roker Park (see page 244) looked very like the main stand at Ibrox, as did the stands at Everton, Plymouth and Portsmouth. This is hardly surprising as all were designed by Archie Leitch.

The exit stairways at Newcastle United's St James' Park were on a slope not unlike those that used to exist behind each goal at Ibrox. However, the stairway design in Newcastle, with turns and crowd-breaks, would have prevented a disaster like the 1971 tragedy in Glasgow.

There is barely an example of an old Scottish ground with twin stands, such as those at Arsenal's Highbury (see next page). Or, at least, nothing on the same scale. These opulent stands are perhaps comment upon the type of London customer The Arsenal hoped to attract.

■ **Left: The Spion Kop at Liverpool's Anfield was probably the most famous terracing in football. In its pomp it held 30,000, until it was demolished and replaced with a stand in 1994.**

Thanks to a quirk of acoustics the steel roof, put on in 1928, seemed to enhance and amplify crowd noise.

There is much debate over this, but Liverpool fans on the Kop began singing Beatles songs in the early 1960s, then changed the lyrics to include the names of players – and modern-day chants and songs at matches, distinct from the singing of traditional songs that had existed before this, started from there.

The Spion Kop terrace was built in 1906, named for a battle six years previously during the Boer War. The British Army were sent to capture a hilltop (kop means hill in Afrikaans) and many of the 300 who died in the attempt were from Lancashire. The terrace is named in honour of fallen comrades. More than 20 English grounds have, or had, Spion Kop ends – the first was at Arsenal's former home, the Manor Ground, in 1904.

In this after-match clean-up photo at Anfield, fires have been lit to burn the piles of litter and the bottom row of crush barriers are closer to the front wall than any seen at a Scottish ground.

■ At first glance this looks like a mirrored image, but these stands at Arsenal's Highbury Stadium faced each other. The West Stand (on the left with the terracing below) was built in 1932 and held 4,000. The East Stand (on the right) was built in 1936. The East was the stand which contained the famous marbled hallways

and bust of legendary manager Herbert Chapman. This photo was taken in 1949 from the Clock End terrace at the south end of the ground. The most vociferous Arsenal fans congregated on the North Bank at the other end. The record crowd for Highbury when it looked like this was 73,295 against Sunderland in 1935.

■ September 27th, 1933. Arsenal v. Rangers at Highbury with the main stand (with its nine-gabled roof) that was the forerunner of the East Stand on the previous page. Gabled stands were the fashion in England for many years, Wolves' Molineux stadium being another famous example. The terraces under these roofs were as normal, although the valleys between the peaks tended to leak.

Arsenal and Rangers played several unofficial "British Championship" games in the 1930s.

The connection between the clubs goes back many years, with a series of games when the London team were known as Woolwich Arsenal and played the first 20 years of their existence at the Manor Ground in Plumstead, south of the River Thames. The club was formed by Fifers who worked at the Royal Arsenal.

In the 1933 encounter on the right, Rangers had beaten the English champions 2-0 at Ibrox the previous week then beat them again, 3-1, on their own ground.

These Rangers-Arsenal "friendly" encounters have been played more than 20 times over the decades. Sometimes, however, relations between the clubs' supporters were rather less than friendly

From 1910, Rangers held shares in The Gunners. The Glasgow club coming to the rescue when – it is said – Tottenham and Chelsea were trying to gain control of Arsenal to put them out of business.

Rangers were gifted more shares in 1930, as thanks for their help 20 years earlier. This connection was ended by the sale of the Arsenal shares (to the wrath of many Rangers fans) in 2012.

Manchester United's Old Trafford on May 8th, 1958, during the first leg of the European Cup Semi-Final against AC Milan, only a few months after the Munich Disaster.

This photo shows long-serving right-back Billy Foulkes making a tackle in front of Old Trafford's main stand, which extended round behind the goal.

The ground had been bombed in 1940 and again in 1941, forcing United to play at Maine Road, the home of rivals Man. City, until 1949 before returning to Old Trafford. However, the roof wasn't fully replaced for another two years.

The "old" Old Trafford record crowd for a Manchester United game was 70,504 against Aston Villa on December 27th, 1920. The current capacity is 74,410, now the huge new stands have been built.

But the ground held 76,962 for an FA Cup semi-final between Wolves and Grimsby Town in March 1939. Wolves won that game 5-0, though they would lose the final 4-1 to Portsmouth.

■ Newcastle United's St James' Park, pictured on a wet day in 1968.

St James' Park suffered for decades because planning permission (due to the proximity of surrounding buildings) for expansion couldn't be obtained. It was, for instance, to have been a 1966 World Cup venue, but the space issues meant it couldn't be brought up to the required standard.

This view shows the ground from the Gallowgate End, the traditional gathering place of the home choir.

The lack of redevelopment made that end a pretty bleak, cold, and wet place at times.

It was a crumbling, neglected wreck. The toilets were rancid, it was often dangerously overcrowded with up to 12,000 crammed in this one end alone.

Spectators today would probably be horrified at the things that were said, the songs that were sung, and the behaviour of those who stood there.

In other words, it was brilliant! A seething, singing, partisan mass of Geordies, with those classic floodlight pylons towering above.

The ground in general, and the Gallowgate End in particular, generated an atmosphere out of all proportion to its size. Despite the lack of a roof to keep the noise in, the Gallowgate was a deafening place. When an important goal was scored it was a battle just to stay alive among the celebrating, jumping, flailing hordes.

The biggest crowd was 68,386 for a league game against Chelsea on September 3rd, 1930. The fans turned out to see their former hero, Scotsman Hughie Gallacher, who had recently been sold to the London club.

As it was designed by the famous Archibald Leitch, it is no surprise that the two-tier main stand at Sunderland's Roker Park looked very like the Struth Stand at Ibrox.

Roker Park was a World Cup 1966 venue, this photo was part of the publicity drive for that tournament.

The names Roker Park, the Roker End, the Fulwell End, the team, the town . . . they are almost the same idea all wrapped up together. Football is an all-encompassing blanket down Sun'lund way. It is an infectious, touching, marvellous thing.

The old Roker Park fitted just over 68,000 Mackems and Geordies in, for a game against local rivals Newcastle in 1950.

It is well over 20 years since it closed, but the legends live on. Indeed, the echoes have barely died away.

CHELSEA

■ Stamford Bridge has several distinctions. It isn't in Chelsea (it is in Fulham), it used to be easily the largest club ground south of the Border, and was laid out quite like Easter Road used to be. It is the only ground in England to have been built first, then have a club founded to occupy it.

The official record attendance is 82,905, Chelsea v Arsenal on October 12th, 1935. The real biggest gate, however, was on November 13th, 1945, for a friendly against Moscow Dynamo.

This was one of the first great post-conflict, imagination-capturing football events. After the lack of football, and the fascination for all things Soviet after their armies had broken the back of the Wehrmacht, thousands of extra spectators gained access by fair means and foul. No one was properly counting.

The attendance for the 3-3 draw was given as 74,496 but more than 100,000 crowded in. Dynamo had a goal disallowed because it had gone in off a spectator standing too close to the byline.

The stadium opened as an athletics venue in 1877, but was bought by businessmen Gus and Joe Mears in 1904. They tried to get Fulham to move in, but when they refused Gus was all set to sell it to a railway company as a coal yard. However, he eventually decided to start his own club, Chelsea FC, and his family retained ownership until his great-nephew sold it to Ken Bates in 1982.

The Mears brothers had intended the ground to be a top-class venue hosting cup finals and internationals – much like Hampden – and it held three FA Cup finals and four England internationals, including the 1913 England-Scotland encounter, before Wembley was built.

Events at these two grounds changed for ever the experience of watching football in Britain.

The fire at Bradford City's Valley Parade (above) happened on the last day of the 1984-85 season at what should have been a celebration of Bradford winning the Third Division title. A discarded match or cigarette started a quickly-spreading blaze in the old wooden stand, which took the lives of 56 fans.

This resulted in the Popplewell Inquiry which changed the design, materials to be used, and safety standards of grandstands.

At Hillsborough (opposite page) four years later, a

total of 97 Liverpool fans were crushed to death at an FA Cup semi-final against Nottingham Forest.

The subsequent Taylor Report made 76 recommendations, including that major stadiums be all-seated, and perimeter fences be taken down. This was made law by the 1989 Football Spectators Act.

The act didn't apply to Scotland, but the SPL made all-seater stadiums a requirement of league membership from 1998.

Some grounds are now putting in place "safe standing areas", with barriers between rows, but a return to the vast old-style terraces is unlikely.

■ **No guide to English grounds could be complete without paying homage to Preston North End's Deepdale. It has hosted football since 1878, the oldest continually-in-use football stadium in England.**

Many of the details of spectators attending football matches were invented at Deepdale (and places like it) in the 1870s.

Nothing like football stadiums existed before this. Preston worked out how to get spectators in, collect an entrance fee from every one, and ensure they could all see the game.

Deepdale's South Pavilion, in the background of this photo, was built in 1934, with the highest attendance (42,684) four years later in a Division 1 game against Arsenal.

The entire ground was redeveloped in the 1990s and early years of this century, with the Pavilion Stand last to fall.

Preston, although now going through leaner times, were giants of the game in the late 19th Century. They won the first Football League in 1888-89 (going undefeated the whole season) as well as the FA Cup.

The club has been at the wrong end of the gradual southernwards levelling of power in the English game. No team south of Birmingham won the league from its inception in 1888 until Arsenal did it in 1931. Since then, London clubs have taken 21 titles, alongside a handful of other southern counties champions.

Dundee

Scottish
Brewers
McLEAN & STEWART
TIMEX
SPICED RUM

DUNDEE'S biggest ever crowd, on February 7th, 1953, came not surprisingly when they had one of their greatest ever teams on the pitch.

In the early 1950s The Dark Blues had one of the world's best players in the shape of inside-left Billy Steel, as well as a contender for the title of Scotland's all-time-greatest goalkeeper in Bill Brown, and the likes of Bobby Flavell in their forward line.

They had won the League Cup in 1952, and would win it again, and be Scottish Cup runners-up, later that 1953 season.

Indeed, the club might well have won the League in 1949, going in to a last day game against Falkirk with a one-point lead but losing the title to Rangers with an out-of-character 4-1 loss at Brockville. The Light Blues did the opposite, recording a 4-1 win at bottom-of-the-table Albion Rovers.

DUNDEE FOOTBALL CLUB LIMITED
GROUND — DENS PARK, DUNDEE
Directors
JAMES R. GELLATLY, C.A. (Chairman)
JOHN R. M. SWADEL, J.P. (Vice-Chairman)
FRANK GRAHAM
ROBERT CRICHTON, C.A. (Secretary)
Manager: ROBERT SHANKLY, Dens Park, Dundee.
Phone 86104

Dundee v. Raith Rovers 31st December, 1960
LEAGUE CHAMPIONSHIP

It pays Dividends to get in touch with
MELDRUMS
SPORTS OUTFITTERS
SUPPLIERS TO THE DUNDEE FOOTBALL CLUB
Club Secretaries should write for illustrated list sent post free
7-9 REFORM STREET, DUNDEE
Phone 24751

All this captured the imagination of football fans in Tayside, Angus, Perthshire, and north Fife. The competition from St Johnstone and close neighbours Dundee United was negligible, both clubs languishing in the B Division. So crowds flocked to Dens.

Dundee's average gate at this point in the 1950s (in a town booming with industrial giants such as NCR and Timex bringing jobs) was comfortably above 20,000 and it looked like the club was at last fulfilling its potential to be a major force in Scottish football.

Regular silverware was in the trophy cabinet and consistent League challenges mounted against Glasgow's big two and the impressive Hibs, Hearts and Aberdeen teams of the era.

The official record crowd came in a Scottish Cup second-round encounter with Rangers that generated gate receipts of £3,270.

Dundee had spent the week at a special preparatory camp in Pitlochry, but no amount of training could change the fact that the Dark Blues' diminutive forward line were out-muscled by the "Iron Curtain" they faced.

The game had been reasonably even until the 59th minute, though the famous description of "defences on top" might well have been applied.

However, this all changed when quickfire goals from Johnny Hubbard and Derek Grierson put Rangers in the driving seat. After that, George Young, Ian McColl and Willie Woodburn – each man a formidable athlete – closed their tall and strong ranks and denied everything the quick, clever, but much shorter and lighter, Dundee forward line could come up with.

Rangers went on to win the Cup that year.

Dens Park at this stage in its history was a good place to watch football.

This was before roofs were put on the Provost Road and Dens Road-side terraces, but Dens was well-known for generating a great atmosphere when a big crowd was in and watching an on-song Dee side.

It is perhaps no surprise then that the official highest attendance probably isn't the true highest attendance. The biggest crowd was most likely four years before the 1953 cup-tie, on Monday, January 3rd, 1949.

With Dundee and Rangers vying for the previously mentioned League title, The Ibrox side came to Tayside as first foots.

Rangers had beaten Celtic 4-0 in the New Year's Day game, while Dundee had taken two points home from Pittodrie with a 3-1 victory the same day. The scene was set for a showdown between the League's top two, and everyone wanted to see it.

The ground filled up quickly until the only turnstiles still open were those at the Dens Road-Provost Road corner of the stadium. Pressure from the restless crowds outside burst open the exit gates and an estimated 2,000 rushed in before police regained control.

Hundreds more scaled the roof of the Thomas C. Keay Engineers and Mill Furnishers factory at the opposite end of the ground and clambered over the fence to gain entry, though many stayed perched on the roof for the duration of the game (much to the dismay of the irate works watchman).

Others climbed the perimeter on the Provost Road side, the few strands of barbed wire on top of the wall being nothing to a crowd of men, most of whom had served in the war or done National Service in which negotiating such obstacles was part of their basic training.

It is impossible to say what the crowd inside Dens was that day. The official attendance went down as 39,975 but it may have been above 45,000 – with an estimated 5,000 still outside.

Such was the crush that the Derry stairway leading to Dens Road was choked with supporters who couldn't squeeze over the brim to the arena itself.

This sparked the unusual scenario of fans asking to get out of a match, but not being allowed to do so as it was feared those still outside would push to get in if a gate was opened.

It is tempting to say that, nowadays, this would have resulted in an ugly scene, but the stoic spectators of 1949 largely accepted the situation and behaved very well as they waited patiently for the crush outside to ease.

And there are no reports of people asking for their gate money to be refunded.

Crowds in those days accepted that, sometimes, it would be impossible to see a game due to the numbers attending.

Urged on by the huge support, Dundee won 3-1, despite losing the first goal, and by the end of the match would top the table with a game in hand.

■ In a scene that could be an L. S. Lowry painting, players help to get a frosty Dens Park playable in 1951.

■ **Another photo of Dens on a snowy day, this time in December 1976 giving a good view of the Provost Road End before it was given bench seats. Like Firhill, this was a terrace with two types of crush barrier.**

■ Dundee, like most clubs, used the layout of their ground for fitness training. This 1950 pre-season training shot shows the players bunny-hopping up the Derry steps, with interested onlookers outside.

■ The Derry gets a brush-up by groundsman Willie Robertson before staging the 1980 League Cup Final. Dundee had installed bench seats earlier that year. The Provost Road End (in the background) would soon follow suit. The physical limitations of a seated area, compared to a standing terrace, are perfectly illustrated. There is a bench on every second or third terrace step in this pic, whereas previously the notional capacity crowd would have been calculated assuming there would be fans standing on every step.

Dundee had originally played at Carolina Port at Dundee Docks. But when the Harbour Trustees decided to expand the port, a new ground was found on what was then the northern outskirt of the town.

Dens Park was opened in 1899, after an initial back-breaking task of converting what had been quite steep-sloped farmland into an almost-flat playing surface.

The club initially leased the land but bought it outright in 1919. At that point it was developed further and a modern stadium emerged.

It was an Archibald Leitch design. His stand (shown on next page) opened in 1921, giving two stands at the ground.

The new stand was one of three Leitch designed with a "crook" to follow the lie of the land (the road outside, where Sandeman Street meets Tannadice Street, in Dens Park's case). The other two, now demolished, were at Wolves and Blackburn Rovers, though Hampden had a slight "turn" too. The Dens stand has a 28-degree turn.

A roof was put on the Derry in 1959, the partial cover on the Provost Road End followed six years later.

Dens was perhaps at its most spruce in the summer of 1962 (when this photo was taken) as the home of the Scottish First Division champions, with an average crowd in the season just finished of almost 16,000.

This shot of Dens Park was taken in 1921 and shows the then new stand on the far side, which isn't quite complete.

The quality of the photo, due to its age, isn't good. It shows, however, the old wooden stand and pavilion (known to Dundee supporters in those days as "the reserve stand") on the south side of the ground.

This stand had originally stood at Carolina Port and had been dismantled and rebuilt up the hill at Dens.

On Christmas Day 1921, fairly soon after this photo was taken, the pavilion and shored-up stand was ruined by fire. The cause was thought to be a discarded cigarette as the blaze started shortly after a Dundee v Hamilton Accies match, though dark rumours of the blaze providing a useful insurance pay-out circulated.

Dundee had, in any case, planned to demolish the structure at the end of that season.

This side of the ground (facing Dens Road) was then built up further to create the high bank of "the Derry" that is still in place.

Going even further back into the history of Dens Park, this is Dundee, the holders at the time, in a Scottish Cup Quarter-Final against Rangers on February 25th, 1911. Dundee won 2-1, but would fall to Hamilton Accies in the semi.

The old north stand had only recently been extended, having previously stopped level with the 18-yard box.

Football grounds were different in those days. There was a perimeter fence, but chairs and benches were placed in front of it all the way round the pitch for this tie, which set a new Dens record attendance of 30,000.

The game they watched was also very different.

Keepers could handle the ball anywhere in their own half (but not carry it). Though this rule would be changed the following season to restrict handling to the 18-yard box.

The offside law required three players to be between the man receiving the ball and the goal line, which meant there were an awful lot of offside whistles. This changed to two players in 1925 and has remained that way.

Players could be offside from a throw-in (this was changed in 1913).

And pitches had no semi-circle on the edge of the 18-yard box (the "D"). They weren't introduced until 1937 following repeated problems and controversies with encroachment at penalty kicks.

■ Dens Park saw heady times in the 1960s. The pic above is 1960, with recently-installed floodlights, and illustrates the line of the “kinked” stand and enclosure in comparison to the pitch. On the right is the European Cup Semi-Final of 1963, when Dundee played AC Milan in front of 38,000.

Hamilton Academical

THE biggest crowd at Douglas Park was 28,690 for a cup-tie against Hearts in 1937. It came, surprisingly, on a Wednesday afternoon.

In the days before floodlights, midweek afternoon games were common with many men having half-days enabling them to get out of work to attend. Though weekday crowds, while still good in those days of very high attendances, were rarely record-breakers.

But Accies had a very good side in the 1930s, led by prolific centre-forward Davie Wilson who scored more than 400 times for the club. They regularly finished in the top half of the First Division and won that game against Hearts 3-1.

The main stand was designed by Archibald Leitch, though is possibly the smallest grandstand of the great designer's career. It was opened in 1913. A small extension was put on in 1989 – that extension is now at Auchinleck Talbot's Beechwood Park.

From 1963 Douglas Park was overlooked by the 17-storey Lanark County Building. With its full-glass walls front and back, it was designed to look like the United Nations HQ in New York City which had been built 12 years earlier. Though Hamilton's version is only a third as tall.

This photo was taken during a 7-1 loss to Rangers on October 30th, 1965 – Accies spent just one season, 1965-66, in the First Division between the mid 1950s and mid 80s.

The site of Douglas Park is now a supermarket. The club had been there since 1888 but played their last game at the old ground at the end of the 1993-94 season. Amid financial and legal wrangling, it took seven years before New Douglas Park opened, with home games played in the intervening period at Firhill or Cliftonhill.

The new ground is just 100 yards from where the old one was.

■ **December 1st, 1973, was one of those bone-chilling days that a Scottish winter can throw at us. The only First Division game that went ahead was Celtic's visit to the seaside at Arbroath, but the TV cameras were at Douglas Park for the Accies-Airdrie Second Division promotion battle. TV gantries weren't part of pre-World War 1 grandstand requirements, so alternative filming arrangements had to be made.**

■ **The clubs were placed first and second in the table, but the game was a disappointing 0-0 on a heavily-sanded pitch that Diamonds boss Ian McMillan described as "farcical". The cameraman on the crane probably found it quite bracing. At the end of that season Airdrie would be Second Division champions, while Accies were third, three points behind runners-up Kilmarnock, and missed promotion.**

■ **Accies v St Johnstone on December 30th, 1978. Saints left-back Tom McNeill heads off the line on another icy Douglas Park surface that – even for the standards of those days – must have been close to unplayable. Accies won 2-1 with goals from Joe McGrogan and an o.g. by Saints' Gordon Hamilton.**

■ Celtic's John Higgins tries to chip Accies keeper Joe (Tiger) Houston during a Scottish Cup tie on March 13th, 1954. The attendance was an all-ticket 22,000, but spectators sat all round the track and there was a panic when a barrier collapsed behind one goal. Celtic, on their way to a League and Cup double, won 2-1.

■ **September 5th, 1953. The Douglas Park main stand makes a dramatic backdrop as Accies' Bobby Cunning beats Celtic keeper Andy Bell to the ball. The stand was 190 feet long, its original capacity was 1,221.**

East Stirlingshire

THE biggest crowd that was ever tempted into Firs Park was a very impressive 10,000 for a Second Division game against St Mirren on November 17th, 1935. Shire won 3-2.

There are claims that a Scottish Cup tie against Partick Thistle in February 1921 drew an even bigger crowd, though details are sketchy.

In any case, anyone who ever visited the ground before it closed in 2008 would wonder how 10,000 ever managed to get in. There were only six turnstiles and one exit gate.

It is another shake-the-head moment when you have to wonder why there weren't more crushing incidents in those far-off days.

The enclosure roof in this photo is the replacement Shire put up after the original one had been carried off to New Kilbowie during the much-hated-by-locals merger with Clydebank in 1965 that only lasted a year.

■ **Right: a proud day for the Falkirk club. February 8th, 1969 – they drew 1-1 with First Division St Johnstone and had good chances to win the Scottish Cup Second Round tie. But Saints won the replay 3-0 and a trip to Celtic Park in the quarters. This was a very cold day, a game played on a hard surface. But Shire keeper Andy Jeffrey's plus-fours and baseball boots still fall into the "don't-see-that-often" category!**

LAND-ROVER

13

Weather

THERE was weather in Scotland in the black and white era, it is fair to say.

And there still is – sun, snow, sleet, hail, ice, rain, fog, haar, wind-storms, you name it. The famous "four seasons in one day" isn't rare. Sometimes you get two seasons both at the same time!

The difference is that in years past, despite having only primitive pitch protection measures, the games were more often played.

There are photos here of matches on surfaces and in conditions no modern referee would dream of declaring playable.

Games are now postponed even if the undersoil heating has kept the surface playable but the stadium approaches are deemed too icy for fans to safely negotiate.

This wasn't even considered in the old days.

■ **Left: 1958. Game off. A view from the main stand at Ibrox that also shows a middle prop many clubs used to ensure their wooden crossbars didn't warp.**

■ **Right: August 30th, 1989, a Skol Cup quarter-final at Pittodrie between Aberdeen and St Mirren. It poured! The Dons swam to a 3-1 win.**

■ **Drookit. A deluge at Dens Park in the 1950s. If puddles weren't too deep, games went ahead. It depended on whether the ball bounced across most of the pitch. And if games started, they were almost always played to a finish. Abandonments for rain did happen, but were very rare.**

■ **Drookit. John Fallon in a Celtic v Dundee game in torrential rain on November 14th, 1964. It got so intense that referee Watson took the players off the field for five minutes because he couldn't see what was happening though the sheets of water coming down. Rain got into the floodlights, popping 22 lamps (of 50) on one pylon, and two or three each on the others. Dundee won 2-0. Hugh Maxwell, a £15,000 buy from Falkirk, made his debut for the home side and (according to Celtic folklore) didn't actually touch the ball!**

■ Sometimes, all you can do is laugh. Dundee's players have a paddle at Somerset Park. Gemme will be on ref, aye? We'll stay in the shallow end.

■ **Two photos from Stranraer, February 8th, 1969. A snell wind whipping hailstones over Stair Park like machine-gun fire. The conditions were described as "ludicrous" in the papers, and you can see why – Stranraer keeper Sandy MacLachlan (and the young lads on the right) don't look like they are enjoying their day much. Morton beat the home side 3-1 in a Scottish Cup tie. Hal Stewart, the great Cappielow impresario, put the win down to his Vikings, Barney Jensen and Per Bartram, being used to such weather.**

A steam train passes Central Park on January 26th, 1963, the worst winter of the 20th Century. This was supposed to be a Scottish Cup Fife derby between Cowdenbeath and Dunfermline.

A local referee declared the pitch playable, but when the match ref arrived he put the game off and the gathering spectators had to be turned away.

Hundreds of pies that the club had already used the gas to heat went to waste. It was a tragedy.

This photo was a "still" produced at the request of ITV's Scotsport, who had intended to show the match. The scaffolding erected on the terracing on the right was to have held the cameras.

■ **Partick Thistle's Firhill, pictured in February 1991, from the now-gone city end terrace. Sometimes the snow was so thick that (very reluctantly) a game just had to be called off.**

Games would go ahead if there was a few inches of snow. Similar to rain, referees declared that if the ball bounced, the surface was playable. Lines were cleared, as seen here, so in/out decisions could be made.

■ **Two photos of Celtic v Dundee United at Celtic Park on December 8th, 1973. It was a 3-3 draw. Above: United keeper Hamish McAlpine snowploughs into a tackle on Bobby Lennox.**

■ **Left: Walter Smith, a Dundee United defender at the time, is booked after a very sliding tackle.**

■ You don't see this much any more. It looks like a curling bonspiel but is actually half-time in the Morton v Killie match of January 19th, 1980. An army of groundsmen brush away snow in an effort to find the lines of Cappielow's 18-yard box. The 2-1 defeat was a severe blow to Benny Rooney's Greenock men, who were challenging hard at the top of the league at the time – though they fell away to a sixth-place finish as Alex Ferguson's Aberdeen stormed to the title.

ABCDEF
GHIJKL
COAL

■ Cappielow again. On February 19th, 1966, every senior game in Scotland was put off due to a nationwide blanket of snow. But Morton and St Mirren braved the conditions to play a friendly. Each player was promised a canteen of cutlery if they won. As it was a 3-3 draw, the clubs decided to play again for the forks and knives the following Wednesday. Yes, football (and footballers) were different in those days.

An ice-breaker sometimes gets things started, but not on this occasion.

This is February 1979, groundsmen George Smith and Jimmy Gibson chipping away at the glacier that covered Muirton Park. But the visit of Dumbarton was still cancelled.

This brought the Pools Panel into play. The panel was made up of former players who decided whether (in their opinion) a game would have been won by the home or away team, or might have been a 0-0 draw or – most valuable of all – a score draw.

The opinions didn't count for points, of course, they were solely intended for pools coupons.

The panel started during the terrible winter of 1963, with former England internationals Ted Drake, Tom Finney, Tommy Lawton, ex-referee Edward Ellis, and former Ranger George Young as the Scottish expert. There were various other famous names on the panel over the years, including another ex-Ranger Ian McColl, and Lisbon Lion Ronnie Simpson.

Rumour had it that the panel members were given generous fees and met to be wined and dined at London's Hilton Hotel or Connaught Rooms.

The panel still sits today, but has been reduced to three members.

■ Perhaps it takes a strange eye to see it, but there is a deeply Scottish, working-class, footballing beauty about this photo of Stenhousemuir v Cowdenbeath on January 15th, 1977. A Division 2 game played in a razor-sharp north wind on an iron-hard surface. 'Beath won 1-0 with a goal from Jim McPaul. The home side's George Bone was booked for throwing a snowball at Cowden's George Hunter. None of the players are wearing gloves, though one of the linesmen is. He must have had flu.

February 1968. You've got to admire this bloke's optimism.

■ And he was right. This was preparation for a crunch Scotland v England Euro Championships game. Hampden was kept under 30 tonnes of straw for four days, while blizzards raged and sub-zero temperatures prevailed. The covering was removed by 125 volunteers on the day of the game and, as luck would have it, a sudden thaw left the pitch very soft. It was 1-1 in front of 134,000. But Scotland needed a win and so failed to qualify for the quarter-finals. Only the last four teams progressed to a finals tournament (in Italy that year) in those days.

■ **November 1969, an upgrade on straw. Ibrox gets hollow boxes that fit together – jigsaw-like – to insulate the pitch.**

■ Due to the way football terrace roofs are constructed, none is invulnerable if a strong enough gale blows in just the wrong direction. The open-front design means they catch the wind like a sail. When a gale is too powerful, bits blow off – as happened at Ibrox on January 15th, 1968, when Hurricane Low Q (the worst natural disaster to hit Scotland since records began) swept in.

Wind can really spoil a game. And a ground. This photo, of Forfar's Station Park, taken on February 5th, 1957, is significant for what is not in it – the roof of the grandstand. It had been blown away by gales the previous night.

■ **The back and front of the ruined Station Park stand. A committee was formed and events – including the sale of the world's largest bridie – were staged to help the club raise cash for a replacement stand. This was opened on January 31st, 1959, and is shown in this book's Volume 2.**

Of all weather conditions, fog was, and still is, the least favourite of fans.

There is entertainment value in a game with players slithering in the snow, struggling through a mud bath, or splashing in puddles. Even the unpredictable bounces of a frozen pitch can be interesting – “a great leveller” they used to say.

Fog means you can’t see anything at all.

Referees ruled that if they could see both goals from the centre-spot, the game went ahead. But the layout of some grounds placed fans 50 yards behind the goal, without a chance of seeing anything at all at the other end of the pitch.

■ **Left: January 11th, 1964. A Scottish Cup tie at Pittodrie between Aberdeen and Hibs in the haar rolling in off the North Sea. It was rumoured that the Dons won 5-2.**

■ **Right: November 21st, 1962. Frank Haffey seemingly alone at Celtic Park during a fog-bound 3-2 win over Rangers in the Glasgow Cup. It was a Wednesday 2.30pm kick-off.**

Worst of all is when you've allowed fans into the ground. This was to be Partick Thistle v Falkirk on February 9th, 1963.

1. The ref declared the game on at 1pm, but an hour later decided the pitch was unplayable. He'd been happy with a game on a frosty surface, but a thaw brought a flood.

2. Groundstaff, players and helpers from the crowd got busy sweeping, forking, and filling wheelbarrows with water.

3. But as soon as one puddle was dealt with, another appeared.

4. It was a hopeless task.

5. The natives grew restless.

6. And gathered outside the main entrance demanding their money back.

7. Rolls of vouchers were hastily found and distributed for entry to another game.

Strangely, the turnstiles counted 4,000 coming in but 4,500 vouchers were claimed on the way out! Clever, these Maryhill folk.

4

5

6

7

A last word on the weather must be said about a cold and foggy afternoon at Ibrox.

These photos show the scenes as Colin Stein's late equaliser goes in on January 2nd, 1971. Moments after this, someone stumbled on Ibrox's Stairway 13, and 66 people would die in the crush.

The disaster, as has been proved, wasn't anything to do with Stein's goal. But when the causes were analysed, was enough attention paid to what the weather conditions had been?

Standing for a couple of hours on a concrete terrace on a cold, damp, January day in Scotland has an effect on a human being. It chills you to the core, stiffening joints and slowing reaction times.

You look forward to hurrying home for a cup of tea, or to a pub for a drap o the cratur. And when people hurry, numbed by the cold, they make mistakes and accidents can happen.

There is little that can be done about the Scottish weather, of course. Except to have it serve as a reminder to take care.

Ayr United

THERE is a lot of affection for Ayr's Somerset Park throughout Scotland. This is because it is one of the last surviving "old" grounds where football can be watched in the traditional way – standing up. It's the one stadium in this book for which a relatively modern pic could be used.

However, it has a highly unusual arrangement of terrace roofs. There are very few other grounds in the UK with a main stand, two covered ends, but an open-to-the-skies long terrace down one sideline.

The stand was built in 1924, paid for by a run to the Scottish Cup Quarter-Final, which required three replays (in front of a lot of paying spectators) before eventual tournament winners Airdrie progressed.

It is one of the relatively few Archibald Leitch designs still in existence and is now close to 100 years old, though got an extension (taking it the full length of the pitch at the east end) in 1989.

A roof was put on the Railway End in 1933, but the Somerset Road End didn't get a cover until 1971.

Somerset Park didn't have floodlights until the relatively late date of 1970. There had been debate with nearby Prestwick over the form lights might take, as the stadium lies in the airport's flight path.

Just over £12,200 of the £18,000 cost of the lights was raised by supporters and traditional pylons were erected, despite the worries of pilots. They were first used for a reserve game on October 8th, 1970 – although only for the last 12 minutes on what was a dull day. The official switch-on was against Newcastle United 10 days later. Ayr won 2-0.

The biggest crowd at Somerset Park was 25,225 v Rangers in a First Division game on September 13th, 1969. Ally MacLeod's infectious confidence – and considerable skills as a manager – had seen Ayr win promotion the previous year, and they started life in the First Division with a superb run of form.

But the size of the attendance for that game was still a surprise. Worried by overcrowding on the seething terraces, the police ordered the turnstiles to close 10 minutes before 3pm, leaving thousands of angry punters still outside trying (and in many cases succeeding) to get in.

Even then, kick-off was delayed as fans spilled over the pitch-side barriers. Many were allowed to sit on the cinder track a few feet from the touchline.

Ayr won 2-1 with a fantastic performance starring Quinton Young.

■ **This photo (very like the one on this book's cover) shows the scene outside the ground on that 1969 day when Somerset Park's biggest ever crowd was recorded. It illustrates perfectly the measures fans would go to in order to get into a game they had travelled to see. The official crowd figure for that game is demonstrably not accurate.**

ON 1/6
SSION 5/-
ADMISSION 5/-

■ United keeper David Stewart sets himself to keep out a shot from Aberdeen's Jim Forrest in a gluepot of a goalmouth at Somerset Park in December 1971, with Archie Leitch's main stand behind him. This was in the days before the "Panda Pen" extension was added. The athletic Stewart, half hidden by the post in this photo, would go on to great things with Leeds United, playing for them in the European Cup Final of 1975.

■ **August 31, 1974. A healthy 16,000 saw Ayr and Rangers fight out a 1-1 draw. Our photographer sneaked round the goalpost to get this shot of Ayr keeper Ally MacLean being given a telling-off by one of Scotland's all-time-great referees, Bobby Davidson, with the crowd in the background. Somerset Park has, like many Scottish grounds, very little space between the spectators and the pitch. This photo gives a rare on-field view of what players mean when they use the phrase: "the crowd is virtually on top of you".**

■ Somerset Park was one of the venues for the Euro under-18s championships in May 1970. These photos are from Scotland's 2-2 draw with Bulgaria. Some of the better known Continental players in that tournament included: France – Raymond Domenech. The Netherlands – Johan Neeskens, Johnny Rep, Willy and René van de Kerkhof. Wales – Leighton James. West Germany – Paul Breitner, Uli Hoeness, Rainer Bonhof.

■ Scotland's U-18s team that day was:

1. Alan Rough (Partick Thistle)
2. Graham McEwan (Queen of the South)
3. Jim Brown (Aston Villa)
4. Ken Watson (Rangers)
5. Ally Robertson (West Bromwich Albion)
6. John Brownlie (Hibernian)
7. Arthur Graham (Aberdeen)
8. Alfie Conn Jr (Rangers)
9. Eric Carruthers (Heart of Midlothian)
10. Graeme Souness (Tottenham Hotspur)
11. Iain Munro (St Mirren)

■ East Germany won the tournament, beating The Netherlands in the final. Scotland beat France in the third place play-off.

CRSMITH

August 3rd, 1985, Ayr United playing Rangers in a pre-season friendly, with young Rangers full-back Hugh Burns getting in a cross in front of the Somerset Park stand. Hugh would later spend a couple of seasons as an Ayr player.

When the stand was opened in the 1920s, the capacity was given as 2,592.

However, it now seats just 1,597 despite the extension which allowed disabled access and added what was said to be 600 seats.

The difference is that the original bench seats allowed more people in, and (this is a matter of plain truth) partly because people were slimmer in those days.

■ September 13th, 1969. Two more shots of Somerset Park's biggest crowd. It was mayhem, with supporters milling round the pitch, unable to find space on the crowded terraces. Eventually, younger fans had to sit on the pitch-side track, very close to play, and the game went ahead. The low, flat roof with people sitting and standing on it (opposite page) is the turnstiles block that is seen being "stormed" on this book's cover.

Greenock Morton

THE day of Cappielow's biggest crowd was almost a century ago – and it was a riot!

On April 29th, 1922, Morton (as they were then) had just won the Scottish Cup for the first, and so far only, time (though they'd go mighty close again in 1948). This brought the Greenock crowd out in force to celebrate. But it was the last day of the season and visitors Celtic were involved in a highly-charged championship battle.

The Celts were a point ahead of Rangers, but had a superior goal average. A draw would do them, while Rangers had to win at Clyde and hope Morton did them a favour.

There were 23,500 in the ground, though this is an estimate, as was common in those days. Official attendances were rarely given by clubs for league games.

The tension among the Celtic support was palpable. There was no radio or internet coverage so no one knew how Rangers were getting on at Shawfield. However, the Greenock lads were in party mood. In the days long before segregation, fights broke out around the ground at half-time with Morton a goal up.

The match ended 1-1, so Celtic won the league. But the violence didn't stop. There were riotous scenes in the streets after the game, with running battles, charabancs stoned, and at least one serious razor slashing incident.

Greenock became no mean city for an evening.

■ Cappielow striker supreme Allan McGraw gets up to score one of the 140 goals he got for Morton in the early 1960s in front of a packed Cowshed – as the enclosure was, and still is, affectionately known.

Decorators.

■ The stand at Cappielow was built in 1931.

It came at the not inconsiderable cost of £10,000 – the equivalent of about £700,000 today. Though the club has had its money's worth as it is still standing.

It originally had wooden benches, but plastic individual seats were installed in the 1990s.

This view of it is from a League game, Morton v East Fife, played on November 4th, 1950, in front of a 16,000 crowd. Morton won 4-2 with Neil Mochan (before his £14,000 transfer to Middlesbrough the following May 8th) getting a first-half hat-trick.

Mochan is shown challenging East Fife keeper Jim Easson.

On the left is Jimmy Philp (No.4) part of the legendary post-war East Fife half-back line of Philp, Finlay and Aitken.

Jimmy Mallon gets in some training during the club's run to the 1963 League Cup Final in front of the Wee Dublin End. It would get bench seats (bought from Rangers, they had been in the Centenary Stand at Ibrox) but no roof when Morton won promotion to the Premier Division in 1978.

Eric Smith keeps in trim with a sprint along the cinder track at the Sinclair Street end of Cappielow in 1970. He was the coach at this point, but would manage the club for a short period in 1972.

THOR
ators.
SCOTCH

■ There was a fairly unusual arrangement of floodlights at Cappielow.

Three rooftop pylons were put up in 1954 at the same time as the Cowshed got its roof. But another light stood on a curiously shaped pylon at the Sinclair Street end.

This photo shows the Morton v Hearts Scottish Cup Second Round tie of Saturday, February 20th, 1965, a thrilling 3-3 draw with a Scandinavian thread running through it.

Hearts' Norwegian maestro Roald Jensen gets in a header, with Ton's Danish defender Kai Johansen half hidden behind Hugh Strachan, and John Boyd looking on.

The Morton goalkeeper is another Dane, Erik Sorensen, with no number on his back, who saved a penalty that day.

He usually (and famously) wore an all-black strip, but a new SFA rule that season insisted that for cup ties goalies had to wear green, yellow or red shirts.

Hearts won the replay 2-0.

■ **Before the cowshed was roofed. Johnny Whigham, getting a shout from legendary 'Ton keeper Jimmy Cowan, watches a header trundle through the mud and past the post.**

CAR CARE

Peterhead

PETERHEAD moved to Balmoor Stadium in 1997, after selling their old ground, Recreation Park, to supermarket chain Safeway (it is now a Morrisons).

It was the right thing to do, financially, as Recreation Park, which opened in 1891, was showing its age. But there are many in the Bloo Toon who think fondly back to the old place which was in a more sheltered location than the often wind-blasted Balmoor.

They left behind the converted (and blue-painted) phone box that was an admittance-fee collecting point, but took the pie stall with them and re-erected it at the new ground.

Recreation Park's record attendance was a Scottish Cup Fourth Round replay against Raith Rovers on February 25th, 1987, when 8,643 were in attendance. It was a thrilling 3-3 draw, following a 2-2 at Stark's Park. Rovers won the second replay 3-0 at neutral Gayfield.

Peterhead were in the Highland League in those days, but the club is now established in the SPFL. There is potential for growth in a town of nearly 20,000 – significantly larger than places that are home to clubs with a much longer history in the national leagues.

■ **Pictures show the old wooden stand at Recreation Park in 1985.**

332

Violence

THERE's no use denying it, Scottish football stadiums have seen some bad crowd behaviour over the decades. The game depicted here was one of the earliest, and worst, examples of crowd disturbances.

It was the Scottish Cup Final replay of April 17th, 1909, at Hampden. There are very few photos of that day still in existence.

The full tale is overleaf.

The worst riot in Scottish football history took place after the 1909 Scottish Cup Final replay between Celtic and Rangers. The final, on April 10th, had been a 2-2 draw, and the replay the following Saturday was 1-1 after 90 minutes, the first time a Scottish Cup Final replay had been a draw. The rules for what happened next weren't clear.

Rangers and Celtic were already the dominant forces in Scottish football, but there was a suspicion that the two clubs looked for ways to play each other time and again, as the big crowds brought in money.

This was when the "Old Firm" nickname started, not because the clubs were firmly expected to challenge for honours, but a tongue-in-cheek accusation they acted as if they were one revenue-generating firm.

So when the replay finished, the players stood about on the pitch (as shown on the previous page). They thought extra time was to be played. In the days before stadium announcements it was only when the corner flags were collected that the crowd realised the game was over. There was to be a third final, with a third entrance fee to be paid.

Outraged fans invaded the pitch and scuffles started with police. Then, to give a modern description, it all kicked off.

The 60,000 incensed fans fought police, and ripped up any part of the stadium they could get their hands on, starting bonfires with the debris.

The religious element to the Celtic-Rangers rivalry hadn't yet developed to a great degree. This was both sides' supporters protesting against the authorities, angry at what they saw as money-grasping.

The battles and fires lasted two hours. The pay booths, goalposts, seats and fences were burned, while fights raged all round the pitch and up and down the terraces as police tried to enforce order and make arrests. When the fire brigade arrived they too were stoned and attacked.

The SFA had to pay Queen's Park £500 for repairs to the stadium.

It remains the only time the competition has been played but the trophy wasn't won by any team. To this day, engraved on the Scottish Cup is "1908-09: cup withheld".

■ **Right: Hampden's turnstiles ablaze in 1909.**

Football hooliganism would raise its head as a problem in Scotland many times over the years.

These photos are from March 31st, 1962, Celtic v St Mirren in a Scottish Cup semi-final at Ibrox.

St Mirren were leading 3-0 with 16 minutes to go when bottle-throwing broke out behind one goal and fans trying to avoid it jumped the wall.

However, fans from the other end also came on to the pitch. Referee McKenzie initially insisted the field should be cleared and play must continue but after five minutes, amid charges by mounted police, he took the players to the dressing rooms.

Celtic's Frank Haffey strode the pitch, angrily ordering supporters back to the terraces (pic opposite).

The chairman of the SFA's Referee's Committee, Peter Scott, took charge of the situation. He said afterwards: "I was determined that we would not bow to mob law. It was a terrible spectacle to see fans whooping with delight when the referee sent the players off the field. It was obvious they thought

the intimidation had succeeded and the tie was to be abandoned."

Celtic chairman Bob Kelly, always regarded as an honourable man, is said to have approached the St Mirren officials and conceded the game.

This was just one example of the behaviour of fans threatening football as a sport.

Several others, involving almost all of Scottish football's top clubs, could have been shown here. This wasn't any one club's problem.

■ Football grounds were very dangerous places in the 1970s. Above: the victim of a thrown bottle during the 1974 Dundee United v Celtic Scottish Cup Final.

■ Right: A none-too-gentle "choke-hold" arrest is made at Hibs v Rangers, Easter Road, August 10th, 1974.

10

An army of police keeps an eye on the Rangers support at Celtic Park on August 25th, 1973.

The costs were (and still are) huge for the numbers of police needed for an Old Firm game.

Around 500 would be on duty in the 1970s, some brought in from neighbouring forces. Many would be paid at overtime rates.

This was all money that went out of the game.

■ Apologies, you'll have had to turn your book on its side again. This is Celtic v Rangers, August 31st, 1985. A negotiation that is above the heads of the crowd. But despite the very real danger of a tanked-up football fan or a large police officer falling on top of them, few in the crowd take their eyes off the game. But then, right enough, it was a tense 1-1 draw – Paul McStay equalising an Ally McCoist first-half strike.

The most infamous violence in living memory was the 1980 Rangers-Celtic Scottish Cup Final riot.

Hampden had recently had track-side mesh fences installed. This led the police to believe it was more likely any trouble would be outside the ground. The majority of officers were deployed there.

A few Celtic youngsters, then many more supporters, climbed the fence to celebrate their club's 1-0 win.

Rangers supporters climbed the barriers at the other end and various charges between the two sides followed. In truth, there wasn't much hand-to-hand combat it was mainly bottles and stones being thrown.

Roughly equal numbers from both sides were on the pitch and the situation wasn't resolved – indeed it looked like worsening – until the arrival of mounted police who scattered the fans with baton charges.

The upshot was a ban on alcohol consumption within football grounds that is still in place.

The following six pages show a series of photos from that day. Most have never before been published.

■ **When the two sides swelled to such numbers on the pitch that a confrontation seemed inevitable, a single line of police stood in the way. They bravely stood their ground but were hopelessly outnumbered. It would be difficult to say which side started the series of charges – both looked keen to "get" the others. It was a hot day, a lot of alcohol had been consumed and there was a feral atmosphere. Anything could have happened.**

24
25
26

O.P. F.C.
19

■ Some arrests were made, but the vast majority of those who were on the pitch never faced retribution from the law.

■ **Mounted officers arrived at last and even the most belligerent, drunken supporter knew better than to get**

in the way of a charging Glasgow police horse line. The fans' attention switched to saving their own skins.

■ Perhaps the most damning thing about the 1980 riot is that it wasn't unusual behaviour. This was the League Cup Final of October 23rd, 1965. Rangers 1, Celtic 2. The only difference was that there were more police inside the ground in 1965 and a full-scale confrontation was averted. But this invasion led to what turned out to be a 10-year ban on any club winning a cup undertaking a lap of honour round Hampden.

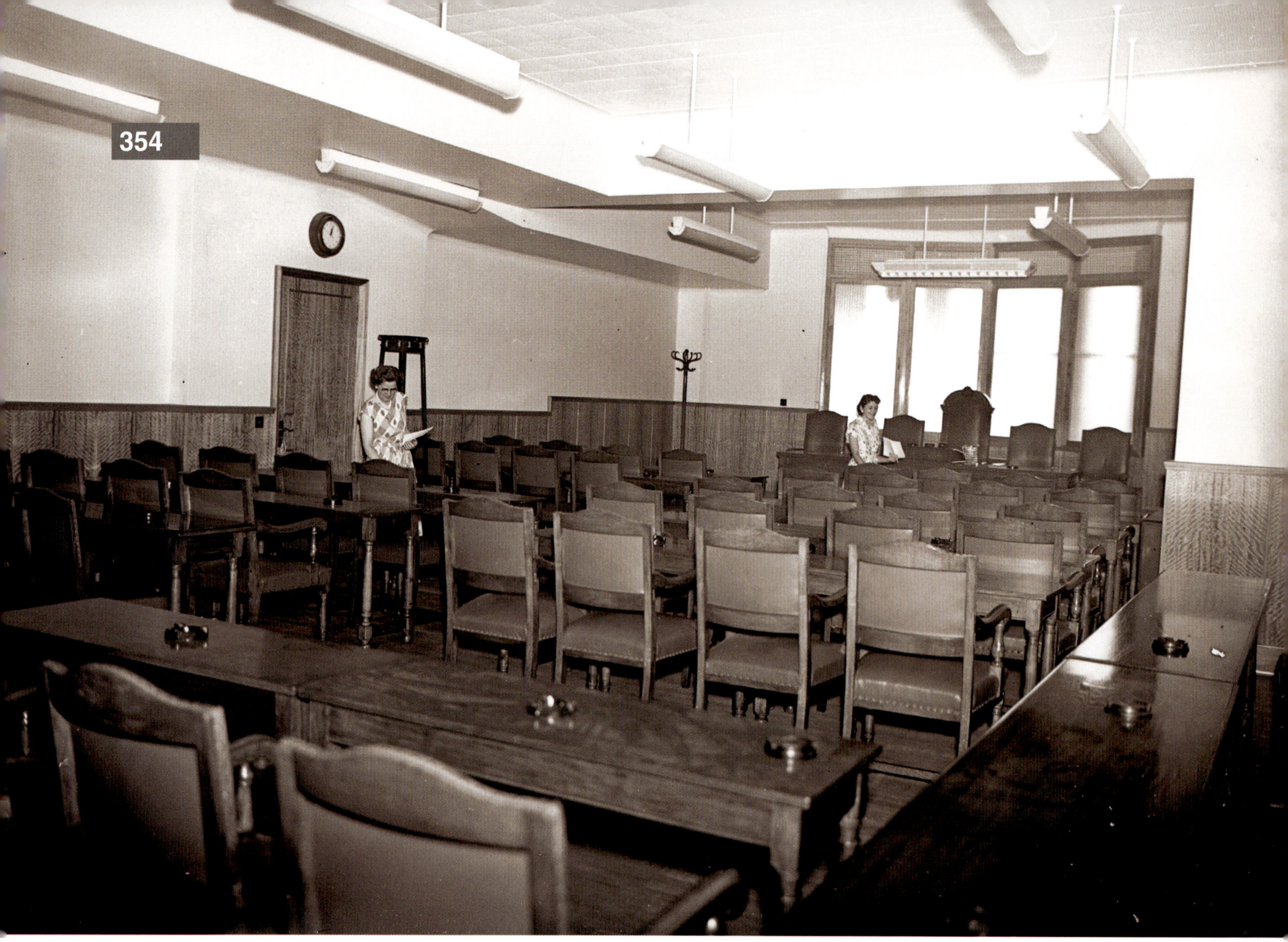

■ Clubs whose fans had misbehaved came here to explain why. This is a rare, possibly unique, photo of the inner sanctum of the SFA at 6 Park Gardens, in Glasgow's West End. It was HQ from 1956 (when this photo was taken) until 2001. This is the main meeting room. The committee sat on the raised dais at the front to hand down their judgements. Note the bar. Alcohol would be banned at grounds, but not at the SFA.

■ Waving a flag is hardly violent behaviour, so perhaps doesn't belong in this chapter. But it was a thing that only really took off in the late 1960s/early 70s. Before then, there would be the odd flag here and there, usually not on a stick, often home-made. But flag-carrying mushroomed until, as can be seen from these Scotland v England 1978 photos, there were tens of thousands of the things. Waving a flag became part of going to the game. This was good news for entrepreneurial salesmen outside the ground, who would charge however much they thought they could get away with – but bad news if you wanted a clear view.

■ Sometimes, you just had to laugh at what went on inside football grounds. Above, a bad lad being frogmarched out of Motherwell's Fir Park (it was May 7th, 1966, the game that clinched Celtic's first league title since 1954). He makes sure to apologise for his behaviour to Jock Stein as he passes by.

■ Right: Brockville 1956. You've got to admire the optimism and sheer gallusness. He is dishevelled, he's had a drink or two, and is in police custody – but he still attempts to chat up a woman in the crowd.

Thanks

THIS book has been the most enjoyable project I've worked on. I came to regard the many people who helped along the way as friends rather than colleagues.

There is nothing better, when doing what is supposed to be work, to find that you've just spent half an hour talking and reminiscing about fitba in the old days – and have forgotten what it was you were talking about in the first place. I am very grateful for the help, advice, expertise, and cups of tea.

The photos in this book are valuable artefacts of Scottish history. I am proud to bring them into the light. This is where I, and hundreds of thousands like me, grew up. We stood on those terraces, we watched our heroes, we enjoyed the experience with our friends and families around us. Going to the fitba in the old days was fantastic. I wish I'd appreciated it more at the time.

Since doing the first *Lifted Over The Turnstiles* book, I have been proud to get out around Scotland to speak to Football Memories groups. There is excellent work being done by an army of volunteers. When I show slides of old grounds and players, it quickly becomes apparent that I am not telling anyone anything – they are telling me! The greatest store of football knowledge that exists is held within the memories of the people who saw it happen. I am extremely grateful to have had some of that knowledge shared with me.

Heartfelt thanks for this, and various other reasons, are due to:

Craig Brown and Leanne Crichton for fantastic, insightful, generous forewords.

Leon Strachan (artist extraordinaire).

John Litster and Jock Gardiner (chief readers. Thanks for saving me embarrassment untold, guys).

Brian Wright (a fitba man of note).

Jim Kidd (almost solely responsible for the "Real Football" chapter).

Jim Burns and Norrie Rush (Hearts info, and lots more. I am truly in awe of their fitba knowledge).

James Coutts, Tony Fimister and Bill Gilby (Raith Rovers).

Bill Lilliman (English photos).

Mike Floate (of footballgroundsfrenzy).

Don Burnett (programmes expert).

David Walker (sports editor of The Sunday Post. Knows his fitba does David).

Joe Bloggs (Celtic Wikki. Good lad).

@StutheJag (Partick Thistle).

Seamus Ferry (Third Lanark).

Paddy Barclay (clever bloke, Paddy).

Tom Purdie (all-round Scottish football knowledge).

John Livingston (Kilmarnock).

The professors of the Old Scottish Football Pictures group on Facebook.

Dave Piggot (for his knowledge of First Aid arrangements at football matches).

Michael White (Falkirk).

Stuart Graham (Motherwell).

David Allan (Cowdenbeath).

Steve Gracie (Dundee United).

Martin Johnston

The Arab Archive.
Peter Hurn (of petespicturepalace)
Norrie Price (Dundee FC).
Doug Nicolson and Duncan McLean (speedway).
David Stuart (Scotland Epistles).
Kevin Robertson (Clyde).
Sue Shepherd (Pittodrie).
Paul Claydon (Groundstastic magazine).
Chris Gavin (Aberdeen).
Dennis McLeary (Berwick Rangers).
Craig Brown (Dunfermline)
Robert Dalzell (Airdrieonians).
Iain Harrison (Hibby).
Duncan Carmichael.
Robert Weir.
Scott Husband.
George Ross.
George Yule.
Douglas Tott.
Chris McNulty.
Ian Moffat.
Ian Stewart.
Alexander Hood.
Colin Robertson.
Rob Casey.
Kevin Robertson.
Alex Holmes.
David Mason.
David Potter.
Iain McCartney.
Uli Hesse.

The DCT archive is where all the gems are hidden. It is curated by a team of clever (and hard-working) people, led by David Powell, and comprising: Barry Sullivan, Gary Thomas, Irina Florian, Kirsty Smith, Katie Thompson, Melissa Lonie, and Mollie Horne.

Publishing a book is a lengthy process with input from many clever people who are very good at their jobs.

Craig Houston.
Gill Martin.
Sylwia Jackowska.
Jacqui Hunter.
Ryan Law.
Connor Vearnals.
Edward Wright.
Julie-Ann Marshall.
Chris Phin.
Nikki Fleming.
James Kirk.

Personal thanks to Carole, Rebecca and Lewis Finan. My family. Thanks for putting up with me and my ever-expanding collection of old football autobiographies.

Bill and Chris Nicoll.
David Patterson (Two Ts – got it right this time mate!)
Bob Seith (even though you don't like fitba!)

My oldest friend Frank Chalmers who went to so many games with me.

Brian Strachan, Doug Robertson, Dave Duncan and Richard Fenton, who shared football with me as a young daftie.

Fraser T. Ogilvie.

And lastly, my father, David Finan (1920-2012). He first took me and my brothers to watch football all those years ago. He started my love affair with the beautiful game. I wish, beyond anything else on earth, that you were still here dad.